WILL TERRORISM END?

THE ROOTS OF TERRORISM

WILL TERRORISM END?

Jeffrey Ian Ross

University of Baltimore

Series Consulting Editors

Leonard Weinberg and William L. Eubank

University of Nevada, Reno

CHELSEA HOUSE
PUBLISHERS
An imprint of Infobase Publishing

Will Terrorism End?

Chelsea House
An imprint of Infobase Publishing
132 West 31st Street
New York NY 10001

Library of Congress Cataloging-in-Publication Data

Ross, Jeffrey Ian.
   Will terrorism end? / Jeffrey Ian Ross.
      p. cm.—(The roots of terrorism)
   Includes bibliographical references and index.
ISBN 0-7910-8310-1 (hardcover)
   1. Terrorism. I. Title. II. Series.
HV6431.R678 2006
303.6'250973—dc22   2006006021

Chelsea House books are available at special discounts when purchased in bulk quantities for businesses, associations, institutions, or sales promotions. Please call our Special Sales Department in New York at (212) 967-8800 or (800) 322-8755.

You can find Chelsea House on the World Wide Web at http://www.chelseahouse.com

Series and cover design by Takeshi Takahashi

Printed in the United States of America

Bang 21C 10 9 8 7 6 5 4 3 2 1

This book is printed on acid-free paper.

INTRODUCTION

Leonard Weinberg and William L. Eubank
University of Nevada, Reno

Terrorism is hard to ignore. Almost every day television news shows, newspapers, magazines, and Websites run and re-run pictures of dramatic and usually bloody acts of violence carried out by ferocious-looking terrorists or claimed by shadowy militant groups. It is often hard not to be scared when we see people like us killed or maimed by terrorist attacks at fast food restaurants, in office buildings, on public buses and trains, or along normal-looking streets.

This kind of fear is exactly what those staging terrorist attacks hope to achieve. They want the public, especially the American public, to feel a profound sense of fear. Often the leaders of terrorist groups want the public not only frightened by the attack, but also angry at the government because it seems unable to protect them from these violent assaults.

This series of books for young people has two related purposes. The first is to place the events we see in context. We want young readers to know what terrorism is about: Who its perpetrators are, where they come from, and what they hope to gain by their violence. We also want to answer some basic questions about this type of violence: What is terrorism? What do we mean when we use the term? Is one man's terrorist another man's freedom fighter? Is terrorism new, a kind of asymmetrical warfare just invented at the beginning of the twenty-first century? Or, does terrorism have a long history stretching back over the centuries? Does terrorism ever end? Should we expect to face waves of terrorist violence stretching into the indefinite future?

This series' second purpose is to reduce the anxieties and fears of young readers. Getting a realistic picture of what terrorism is all about, knowing what is true and what is not true about it helps us "get a grip." Young readers will learn, we hope, what constitutes realistic concerns about the danger of terrorism versus irrational fear. By understanding the nature of the threat, we help defeat one of the terrorists' basic aims: spreading terror.

The first volume in the series, *What is Terrorism?*, by Leonard Weinberg and William L. Eubank, begins by defining the term "terrorism," then goes on to explain the immediate aims and long-term objectives of those who decide to use this unconventional form of violence. Weinberg and Eubank point out that terrorism did not begin with the 9/11 attacks on the United States. In fact, terrorist violence has a long history, one the authors trace from its religious roots in the ancient Middle East up to current times.

For those who believe that terrorist campaigns, once started, are endless, Jeffrey Ian Ross's *Will Terrorism End?* will come as a useful antidote. Ross calls our attention to the various ways in which terrorist episodes have ended in the past. Many readers will be surprised to learn that most of the terrorist organizations that were active in Latin America, Western Europe, and the United States just a few decades ago have passed from the scene. For example, the Irish Republican Army (IRA), long active in paramilitary operations in Northern Ireland, is now in the process of turning to peaceful political participation.

Between accounts of the beginning and end of terrorism are books that approach the problem in two different ways. Dipak K. Gupta (*Who are the Terrorists?*) and Assaf Moghadam (*The Roots of Terrorism*) answer general questions about the origins of terrorists and terrorist organizations. Gupta provides profiles of individual terrorists and terrorist groups, in addition to exploring the issues that inspire terrorists. Moghadam, on the other hand, is more concerned with the organizational and social roots of terrorism. For example: What causes people to join terrorist groups? What are the grievances that often give rise to terrorist campaigns?

While Gupta and Moghadam examine the roots of terrorism in general terms, Jack Levin and Arie Perliger's books each have a specific geographic focus. Levin's *Domestic Terrorism* brings the story close to home by describing domestic terrorist activity in the United States over the last half century. Perliger's book, *Middle Eastern Terrorism*, offers an account of terrorist activity in the region of the world with which such violence is most closely identified.

Finally, we believe that young readers will come away from this series of books with a much clearer understanding of what terrorism is and what those individuals and groups who carry out terrorist attacks are like. ■

CHAPTER 1

INTRODUCTION

Current events, particularly the attacks of September 11, 2001, and the subsequent war in Afghanistan and Iraq, have prompted the general public, the media, and many politicians to think that oppositional (i.e., against the state) political terrorism is not only a relatively new phenomenon, but that it is here to stay.[1] During the past decade, the number of suicide bombings (a highly visible act of terrorism) has increased, attacks are more severe and deadly, and a number of previously unknown terrorist groups have formed. At the same time, a considerable number of potential and actual targets are now better protected; counterterrorist agencies have integrated new safeguards and technologies into their repertoire; cross-agency and cross-national cooperation has improved; and more security policies and practices (e.g., at airports, schools, and workplaces) have been implemented to prevent terrorism or to better respond to it when it occurs. Perhaps what is different is the fact that the events of 9/11 have fostered a change in America's response to terrorism.

BACKGROUND

After the fall of the Berlin Wall (November 9, 1989), the collapse of the Soviet Union (1991), the Persian Gulf War (1990–1991), the election of Nelson Mandela (1991), the signing of the Oslo Peace Accords between Israel and Palestine (September 13, 1993), and the "Good Friday Agreement" between the Provisional Irish Republican Army and the British government (1998), a number of issues that had previously led to persistent political violence abated.[2] In addition, the capture of the heads of significant terrorist movements, such as Abimael Guzman of Peru's Shining Path (September 12, 1992) and Abdullah Ocalan of the Kurdish Workers Party (PKK) (April 15, 1998), led policymakers and political leaders to believe that terrorism was abating. Finally, it appeared as if the world's global economy improved, thus bringing wealth to many individuals, states, and regions. Consequently, many observers and analysts hoped that oppositional political terrorism was a thing of the past, and that it might even end.

The relatively recent Oklahoma City bombing (April 1995), the sarin gas attack in the Tokyo subway (March 1995), and frequent suicide bombings by Hamas in Israel garnered renewed interest in terrorism among a variety of political actors. Then came the 9/11 terrorist attacks, when four planes were hijacked by members of Osama bin Laden's al Qaeda network. The planes slammed into the World Trade Center, the Pentagon, and a rural field in Pennsylvania, causing close to 3,000 deaths and injuring more than 6,300 people.

In the meantime, the new terrorist groups that have formed over the past decade have acquired and used new and more destructive technology in their communications and attacks. At the same time, however, other terrorist groups have disbanded. Finally, reports of poor collaboration among key federal agencies (such as the FBI, CIA, and INS) and U.S. allies came to light during investigations into the causes of the events of 9/11. These reports have indirectly led to both a sense of vulnerability in the United States and elsewhere, and to the establishment of the U.S. Department of Homeland Security.

THE UNIQUENESS OF THE SEPTEMBER 11, 2001, ATTACKS

The 9/11 attacks were, without a doubt, unique.[3] Few incidents of terrorism can compare to the level of horror and the number of people injured and killed. This act of political violence and crime killed more people than the Japanese attack on Pearl Harbor during World War II.

How Events Unfolded

The 1993 World Trade Center Building Bombing as Prelude

New York City's World Trade Center was a symbol of American capitalism and progress, both of which are hated by fundamentalist Muslims, Osama bin Laden, and al Qaeda, bin Laden's organization.[4] On February 26, 1993, Ramzi Yousef and accomplice Mohammad Salameh drove a rented Ford Econoline van laden with explosives to the basement parking lot of the World Trade Center and detonated it. Six people were killed and 1,042 were injured. According to Simon Reeve, author of *The New Jackals,* the incident led to

> more hospital casualties than any other event in domestic history apart from the Civil War. Many of those who escaped without apparent physical injury will be scarred mentally for life, and yet it is almost miraculous that in such a huge bomb attack even more were not killed or injured.[5]

New York City police and firefighters inspect the bomb crater in the garage of the World Trade Center on February 27, 1993, one day after the explosion set off by two men linked to al Qaeda.

Later, on August 7, 1998, bin Laden and al Qaeda were implicated in the bombing attacks on American embassies in Nairobi, Kenya, and Dar es Salaam, Tanzania, which killed 237 and injured 5,000 people—not only Americans, but also citizens of Kenya and Tanzania. On October 12, 2000, al Qaeda allegedly bombed an American naval ship that was docked just off the port of Aden, Yemen. The bombing of the USS *Cole* caused 17 deaths and 30 injuries. Despite international arrest warrants for bin Laden and several other members of al Qaeda believed to be responsible, the United States and other participating countries were unable to capture them.

Ignoring the Signals From Within

As the pieces of the puzzle began to fit together, it became clear that those plotting the 9/11 attacks had been in the United States for a considerable period before the event, undetected by law enforcement authorities and national security agencies. Maybe American security intelligence was blindsided by the

Significant Dates in the History of al Qaeda and the Life of Osama Bin Laden

December 1979: Soviet Union invades Afghanistan. Young Muslim fundamentalists from around the world join forces with Mujahadin rebels to fight guerrilla-type insurgency against the Soviets. This campaign receives covert support from the United States.

February 1989: Soviets are defeated and pull out of Afghanistan. The Taliban achieves power.

August 1990–April 1991: Gulf War is waged. The United States fails to remove its troops from Saudi Arabia.

February 26, 1993: Al Qaeda members Ramzi Yousef and accomplice Mohammad Salameh drive a rented van, laden with explosives, into the basement parking lot of the World Trade Center in New York City. The van explodes, killing 6 people and injuring 1,042.

August 7, 1998: Al Qaeda bombs American embassies in Nairobi, Kenya, and Dar es Salaam, Tanzania, killing 237 and injuring 5,000 people—not only Americans, but also citizens of these countries.

October 12, 2000: Al Qaeda allegedly bombs the USS *Cole*, an American naval ship docked just off the port of Aden, Yemen, causing 17 deaths and 30 injuries.

September 11, 2001: Nineteen al Qaeda hijackers commandeer four airplanes, crashing two into the World Trade Center (New York City), one into the Pentagon, and another, probably headed for another Washington-area target, into a rural field in Pennsylvania.

activities of the 19 or more hijackers because of a focus on other issues or crises.[6] More than likely, there were numerous security glitches; we have since identified counterterrorist measures that should be implemented. Many of these issues were eventually discussed during the meetings of the 9/11 Commission, the group charged with investigating those attacks, which was widely covered in much of the spring 2004 domestic news.[7]

Pet Hypotheses and Theories

Immediately following the attacks, the public, pundits, and experts offered their own hypotheses and theories about what prompted the disaster. Explanations ranged from the simplistic to the complex, from irrational to rational; some individuals relied on history; others invoked the supernatural.

Several questions were raised. Were foreign governments involved? For example, it was suggested that Saddam Hussein, then president of Iraq, assisted bin Laden in his efforts. Could it be that unsuspecting Americans or foreigners unwittingly helped the hijackers? If so, was there something they could have done to prevent the attacks? Since the incident, the public has learned that some of the terrorists received instruction from U.S. flight centers and some even considered using crop dusters to spray an area with chemical or biological weapons. Americans, made wiser by the incident, wonder how these strange occurrences slipped by them unnoticed.

EFFECTS

The 9/11 attacks had both structural and psychological effects.[8] In general, terrorism affects five different political actors: terrorists, victims, the public, businesses, and government. Each one responds differently to terrorist events, and synergistically to each other.[9] In particular, the incident reinforced the vulnerability of the United States and its susceptibility to international terrorism. Although Americans have been the victims of terrorist attacks abroad, rarely have they been targeted by international terrorists at home.

In the aftermath of 9/11, U.S. national security and law enforcement agencies launched a massive counterterrorism effort, supported by legislation in the form of the USA Patriot Act. September 11 has sufficiently seared the public's conscience; it put unprecedented levels of pressure on politicians and practitioners, domestically and abroad, to develop a more focused and realistic approach to preventing terrorism.[10] The United States declared war on terrorism and sent troops overseas, ostensibly to hunt down those responsible for the attacks. Meanwhile, the American public has been faced with bomb scares, breaches of airline security, videotapes of bin Laden and high-ranking members of al Qaeda celebrating the attacks, and other intimidating threats, since September 11.[11] These events have caused many to question the current state of national security.

Many people criticize the inconvenience of heightened security measures at airports, especially in light of ongoing news reports about lapses in such security. The public understandably questions the effectiveness of the new security measures enacted across America and around the world, and wonders if we are truly any safer than before. In short, many people are left with an all-consuming fear. The public still worries about working or living in tall buildings, such as the Empire State Building in New York and the Sears Tower in Chicago, or about using airplanes as a means of transportation.

The "Threat of the Week" Syndrome

In the days and months following the 9/11 attacks, the American public was also subjected to the "threat of the week" syndrome. Shortly after 9/11, numerous rumors surfaced, facilitated by media attention and increased public access to the Internet, about possible terrorist attacks on the United States. Many of these stories turned out to be false. Some of the rumors clearly originated in the minds of a public motivated by fear; others were manufactured by mean-spirited citizens; and a few can be traced to intelligence collected by the government.

What Are the Short- and Long-Range Effects of the 9/11 Attacks?

Although much has been written about the effects of terrorism,[12] and about efforts to combat it,[13] a big picture of the responses to 9/11 had not been developed until recently. Perhaps governments and citizens can do very little to stop attacks, especially when individuals like those involved in the 9/11 attacks are so committed to their cause. Maybe no antiterrorist agency can ultimately deter a determined individual or group of individuals.

America has suffered domestic terrorist attacks in the past (e.g., the Oklahoma City bombing) as well as attempted and successful assassinations of political leaders (e.g., John F. Kennedy and Martin Luther King, Jr.). After each event, government agencies have put into place a new series of countermeasures. Perhaps, however, these responses are obsolete in an age of more sophisticated technology for weaponry and communication.

Immediately after the airliners crashed into the World Trade Center and the Pentagon, the United States went into a lockdown situation. Planes were grounded and trains stopped running. When organizations and governments increase security, they traditionally resort to "target-hardening"—using more blast-resistant materials, architectural designs that can withstand the impact of a highly charged bomb, and blast-resistant barriers. Since the 1960s, the United States and many other countries have taken measures to prevent attacks from occurring and have instituted safeguards to minimize damage. During the 1960s, as a response to highjackings, sky marshals (a program that expanded in the wake of 9/11) were used to protect civilian aviation from this kind of activity, and the number of metal detectors and luggage inspections in airports increased, in order to prevent hijackings.

Passengers remove their coats at a security checkpoint at Seattle-Tacoma International Airport. New security measures, including requiring passengers to remove their coats before passing through metal detectors, went into effect in September 2004. This is just one example of how terrorism within the United States has affected Americans.

Unintended Consequences

Maybe, despite media reports to the contrary, the events of 9/11 are behind us. Bin Laden and his organization have made their point, and, despite their "saber rattling" and the American military and homeland security response, realistically we have nothing more to fear from al Qaeda. Even if this were true, however, the attacks may have served to embolden other individuals or organizations to engage in so-called "copycat acts" of terrorism. Everyone is quick to blame al Qaeda for every terrorist attack since 9/11; this process of contagion is well-known to terrorism experts.[14] We have not heard much lately from right-wing organizations, such as the Aryan Nations, though, and this may be an opportune time for them to step back into the spotlight. Leaders or members of these groups may ride the coattails of increased anti-Arab sentiment in America to achieve a measure of respect among some more conservative citizens.

WHAT CAUSED THE FEAR?

As a result of 9/11, in some quarters, life has changed drastically, although it appears to be "business as usual" in others. These different reactions depend on a number of factors, including proximity to the attacks, the pervasiveness of existing fear in the population, the susceptibility of the actor, and media satura-tion. These factors are discussed in greater detail below.

Proximity and General Level of Fear in the Population

The results of a 2001 University of Houston poll indicate that those who were in closest physical proximity to the 9/11 attacks experienced the highest levels of anxiety. Thus, residents of New York City—even if they did not personally know someone who perished in the tragedy—experienced disruption in some shape or form because of job loss, transportation delays, the massive clean-up, or the much-publicized debate over what to do with the site where the twin towers once stood.[15]

Then again, perhaps some people are still in a state of denial, blocking out the shocking reality of what transpired. Maybe, in an attempt to deal with the horror, Americans have become numbed or have subconsciously numbed themselves. In contrast, some rural communities (particularly those in the West) have encountered virtually no reported increase in anxiety levels. The local sheriff or small-town police officer still does his or her rounds without a glimmer of trepidation that a terrorist plot might be uncovered.

Another rarely examined factor related to fear is age. Those who are young and have no memory or experience with similar tragedies may have a difficult time placing the events of 9/11 into context. Thus, their susceptibility to fear or fear-inducing messages may be high—they think that similar events may happen very soon.

The Government Response to Threats After 9/11

The federal government issued its highest security threat in February 2003 after identifying what it called "credible threats of terrorism." The increased threat came almost simultaneously with the release of a videotape of bin Laden exhorting his followers and those sympathetic to al Qaeda to launch suicide attacks against the United States if it intervened in Iraq. This was also the first time that the federal government suggested practical measures that Americans could take in order to protect themselves, beyond simply being vigilant. In the event of a nuclear, chemical, or biological attack, Americans were advised to use duct tape and plastic on their doors and windows, and have on hand a three-day supply of food. Many commentators and pundits thought this advice was a little unrealistic and impractical, but it did serve as a wake-up call for some Americans, who had not already taken action in the face of increased terrorist threats.

The Department of Homeland Security, in a scene reminiscent of the old days of Cold War nuclear threats, came up with a color-coded method of notifying the public about potential threats and assisting them in being able to judge their seriousness. The system, however, quickly became tiresome; the public had a hard time figuring it out, and it was easily dismissed as ineffective. Even the irreverent and popular *Saturday Night Live*, a weekly television comedy show, spoofed this issue.

Unfortunately, these announcements quickly grew to resemble "the little boy who cried wolf." Warnings would be issued, but no terrorist event—or even a foiled attempt—would take place. In the meantime, the public became desensitized and let its guard down. The government, however, is in a "damned if you do, damned if you don't" situation; it must issue these warnings because it wants to maintain legitimacy. The state must err on the side of caution, but increasingly the warnings, and the officials who issue them, lose legitimacy as the warnings become "background noise" amid the pressures of daily life.

The Media's Role

One cannot pick up a newspaper or watch or listen to a newscast without seeing or hearing some reference to terrorism. The mass media is an extremely powerful player in the dynamics of terrorism.

The Power of the Media

The power of the media has been clearly and unmistakably identified by several researchers and observers of the press. Arno, for example, says,

> Systematic, purposive involvement in conflict situations is the most immediately salient feature of the anatomy and behavior of the news media in relation to other contemporary social entities. They insert themselves or are drawn into virtually every kind of conflict because, in a basic sense, conflict is news.[16]

Communication about certain kinds of issues creates, intensifies, or diminishes conflict.[17]

How Did the Media Become So Important?

Terrorists are acutely aware of the media's unquestionable power. Because of increased competition for our attention, the terrorist events that we notice appear to be, and most likely are, carefully planned in order to capture considerable public attention.[18] In some respects, the growth of terrorism has paralleled the invention, manufacture, and purchase of new technologies.

The media–terrorism connection has much to do with the invention of the printing press and broadcast technologies (radio and television), and the launching of communication satellites.[19] New technologies (e.g., faxes, cell phones, and the Internet) allow the news media to report more quickly, more accurately, and in more depth.

Analyzing the Power of the Media

Intimately connected to terrorism is the power of the media[20] in communicating insurgent messages, affecting audience perceptions, and influencing others to engage in particular terrorist or supportive behaviors.[21] Many terrorist groups know how to achieve media attention. They are very sensitive to the timing of news stories and audience dynamics, and they structure their actions with this in mind. Some terrorist organizations have temporarily taken over media outlets or own their own media sources. Although the members of the media do not cause terrorism, they certainly facilitate the dissemination of information about it.

Crime-Reporting Waves

The phenomenon called "crime-reporting waves" partially informs our perception of terrorism. During the 1980s, Mark Fishman introduced and documented the phenomenon that became known as crime-reporting waves.[22] He demonstrated that the official crime rate, which has been acknowledged to be an inaccurate indicator of actual crime, bears little relationship to how often the media reports on crime. More important, most people derive their fear and safety not from the actual incidence of crime, or from being personally victimized by crime, but rather from the frequency and attention paid to crime in media reports. Simply put, if the media pays considerable attention to terrorism, then viewers will feel frightened.

Building on Fishman's work, others, such as Joel Best[23] and Philip Jenkins,[24] have sensitized us to the fact that, although there may be a very real problem with social predators, such as child molesters or serial killers, the media attention and the public fear that this phenomenon generates is largely out of proportion to the actual number of these types of criminals in society. In short, the public's fear and safety is directly connected to what they read in the press or hear or see in the media.

TERRORISM IS NOT A NEW PHENOMENON

Terrorism in response to some political power or ideology is not a new phenomenon. This type of political violence and crime has occurred since the dawn of human history. The nature of this form of political conflict has changed over time, though, evolving from localized and domestic activities to regional and international events.[25] Consequently, terrorism has become an experience shared by many individuals, organizations, and states.

We can identify the following three dominant periods in the history of terrorism: ancient, modern, and contemporary. These periods encompasses terrorism motivated by religious, nationalist-separatist, and ideological concerns.

Ancient Terrorism

The earliest time frame, the ancient one, covers A.D. 66–1870. Two major terrorist groups were active in the ancient period: the Sicarii and the Assassins. Some of the more notable features of these groups include the facts that, when compared to contemporary terrorist organizations, these "lasted longer," were "responsible for much greater destruction," and were "more religious in character."[26]

Modern Terrorism

The second historical stage in terrorism took place roughly between 1871 and 1960. Several organizations—the majority of which had leftist sentiments and fleeting existences—began their activities during this period. Groups that operated in this era include, but are not limited to, the Narodnaya Volya, anarchist groups, the Social Revolutionary Party, and radical national-separatist groups in Ireland and Armenia.

After World War I, terrorist operations "were mainly conducted by right-wing and nationalist-separatist groups. Sometimes these groups were both right-wing and separatist, as in the case of the Croatian Ustacha, which received most of its support from Fascist Italy and Hungary."[27] During the 1920s, terrorism was a tactic employed by budding nascent fascist groups that were emerging throughout Europe in Germany, France, Hungary, and Romania.[28]

The Sicarii: One of the First Recognized Terrorist Organizations

Originating in A.D. 66, the Sicarii were a religious sect active in the Jewish Zealots' (i.e., rebels) struggle against the Roman occupation in Palestine (modern-day Israel). During this time, the Roman Empire included the Fertile Crescent (the modern-day countries of Israel, Jordan, Lebanon, Syria, Iraq, and Egypt). The Sicarii were extremist, nationalist, and anti-Roman. This organization took its name from the word *sica*, the daggers members concealed underneath their robes and used to assassinate their victims. They killed Jews and Romans—including anyone sympathetic to the Romans or antagonistic to the Sicarri. They destroyed the house of Anaias, the high priest; the palaces of the Herodian rulers; and the public archives. Their commitment to their cause was so great that they even destroyed Jerusalem's food supply in order to motivate those remaining to fight against the Romans in their siege rather than negotiate with them. In A.D. 70, with the Romans on their heels during a siege of Jerusalem, the Sicarii and other Zealots escaped to the deserted fortress of Masada, near the Dead Sea. They were able to defend themselves there for a time, but the Romans finally captured the fort and found many of its inhabitants had committed suicide. The Sicarii ceased activity in A.D. 73.

Contemporary Terrorism

Terrorism taking place in the period from 1960 to the present can be called contemporary terrorism. Since 1968, there has been a sustained increase in the number of terrorist incidents taking place and the number of terrorist groups formed in a variety of countries.[29] Terrorism during this period has been more violent (as measured by the number of individuals injured and killed). Many new groups are better organized and more sophisticated than those in previous historical eras. Terrorism after the early 1960s is also better documented and studied. Moreover, today there is more public, political, and national security awareness of terrorism.

In general, we can divide the history of terrorism during the past four decades even further, into three overlapping periods. Groups are more-or-less revolutionary/nationalist-separatist, left-wing, or right-wing in their ideologies.

The 1960s–1970s

During the 1960s, many groups that were part of larger countries and that had strong nationalist sentiments became increasingly outspoken. Some among their ranks resorted to violent political actions, including terrorism. Among the nationalist-separatist groups, there are right- and left-wing terrorist organizations.

Revolutionary/Nationalist-Separatists

In Canada, the Front de Libération du Québéc (FLQ) operated from 1962 to 1972. This was primarily a nationalist-separatist organization with left-wing sympathies that wanted the predominantly French-speaking province to break away from Canada and establish a fully autonomous, socialist state. This group was responsible for numerous bombings, as well as the well-publicized kidnapping of James Cross and the murder of Pierre Laporte.[30]

In 1964, the Palestine Liberation Organization (PLO) formed. Under this umbrella structure, a number of terrorist

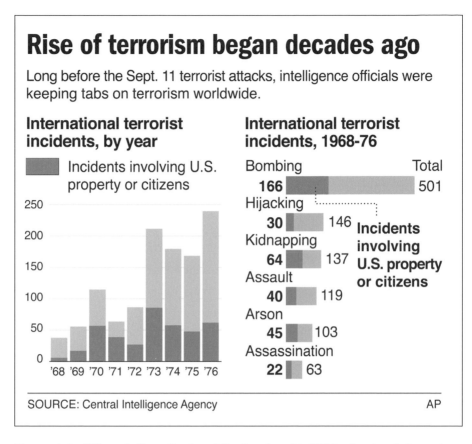

Rise of terrorism began decades ago

Long before the Sept. 11 terrorist attacks, intelligence officials were keeping tabs on terrorism worldwide.

International terrorist incidents, by year

▮ Incidents involving U.S. property or citizens

International terrorist incidents, 1968-76

Bombing		Total
166		501
Hijacking		
30	146	Incidents involving
Kidnapping		U.S. property
64	137	or citizens
Assault		
40	119	
Arson		
45	103	
Assassination		
22	63	

'68 '69 '70 '71 '72 '73 '74 '75 '76

SOURCE: Central Intelligence Agency   AP

Figure 1.1 Although the attacks of September 11, 2001, stand out, terrorism had been a concern long before the twenty-first century. The graph on the left shows how many terrorist incidents occurred each year between 1968 and 1976. The graph on the right breaks down the statistics according to the method used to commit the attacks.

groups took action in Israel, including the Popular Front for the Liberation of Palestine (PFLP). In the aftermath of the 1967 "Six-Day War," George Habash and Wadi Haddad, trained as physicians, founded the PFLP. The organization was based on a number of political groups that had been in existence since the late 1940s.[31] The PFLP had a Communist orientation similar to that embraced by Cuba, Vietnam, North Korea, and the left-wing terrorist forces in Western Europe with which it cooperated. It also considered the Arab middle class to be an ally of Zionism (a philosophy which advocates the existence of a Jewish state), and encouraged war against them.[32] This group received support from the Soviet Union and from other communist countries, and was distrustful of Yasser Arafat, the head of the PLO. Later, it included as many as eight guerrilla organizations. In 1969, Yasser Arafat's revolutionary group, Fatah, gained control of the PLO. In 1972, Black September, another Palestinian terrorist organization that formed in Jordan, began to launch attacks against Israelis and Jordanian political leaders. This group was responsible for the murder of 11 Israeli athletes and one German police officer at the Munich Olympics in September 1972.

During the 1960s, and to this day, the Provisional Irish Republican Army (PIRA) (more commonly referred to as the IRA) in Northern Ireland has carried out attacks against Protestants living there and against Great Britain.[33] In 1975, the Armenian Secret Army for the Liberation of Armenia (ASALA), a Marxist group, formed with the goal of striving for the independence of Armenians in Turkey. The ASALA was responsible for a number of embassy seizures and plane hijackings and was most active in the United States, Canada, and Europe.

Within the United States, some immigrants and foreigners have been playing out their homeland tensions. Over the past four and a half decades, we have experienced instances of terrorist activity from groups sympathetic to the people of Armenia, Croatia, Cuba, and Puerto Rico.

Left-Wing/Revolutionary/Anarchist Terrorism

During the 1960s and 1970s, several left-wing terrorist organizations formed in the United States. Among the most prominent were the Weather Underground, the United Freedom Front, the Symbionese Liberation Army, and Black Militant (e.g., Hanafi Muslim Group). In Europe, the Red Brigades, the

A Comparison Between Left- and Right-Wing Ideologies and Parties

OBJECTIVES	
LEFT-WING	**RIGHT-WING**
More government intervention, particularly in the economy (e.g., more taxes)	Less government intervention (e.g., lower and/or fewer taxes)
More equality	Protection of individual liberties
Pro-choice on abortion	Anti-choice on abortion
Pro-affirmative action	No racial or gender based quotas
More gun control	No gun control
Support environmental protectionism	Oppose environmental protectionism
Anti-death penalty	Pro-death penalty
Increased public funding of social services	Pro-free market
POLITICAL PARTIES	
LEFT-WING	**RIGHT-WING**
Democratic Party	Republican Party
Liberal Party	Conservative Party
Green Party	Libertarian Party
Socialist Party	Christian Coalition
Communist Party	
Progressive Party	

Figure 1.2 Most political ideologies, political organizations, and parties want change (or progress), but they vary on the methods for achieving it and the pace at which it is achieved (i.e., incremental, radical, or extreme). The top table shows some of the most common objectives attributed to each political side, while the second table shows which political parties are commonly associated with each side.

Baader-Meinhoff Gang/Red Army Faction, and Direct Action (Action Directe) came on the scene. In Japan, the Japanese Red Army was involved in many domestic and international terrorist events.

Right-Wing Terrorism

There is a long-standing tradition of right-wing violence in America and elsewhere. Some of the more dominant groups to engage in terrorist acts include the Ku Klux Klan and the Aryan Nations. In Italy, the New Order, the National Vanguard, and the National Front were active during the 1980s.

CONCLUSION

Clearly, individual experiences with terrorism and proximity to the 9/11 attacks had an effect on people's general level of fear. Also important was the media interpretation of the events. It must be understood that terrorism is not a new phenomenon. That is not to say that terrorism won't end, however, because terrorist groups can, and do, disband.

CHAPTER 2

TERRORISM WILL END:
GROUPS THAT DISBANDED OR WERE DECIMATED

The argument that terrorism will end is supported by facts: some terrorist groups have disbanded; terrorism has declined in some countries; and most governments have increased their security precautions in the wake of the 9/11 attacks, making terrorism a less effective tactic. Better security has led to several arrests and the seizure of assets used to support terrorist activities, thus paving the way for legitimate political parties to form. Over the history of terrorism, far more groups have disbanded or were decimated because of the overwhelming power of governments, than have gone on to form legitimate political parties. As governments have become more powerful and have coordinated better intelligence domestically and internationally, there is less room for rogue groups to flourish.

TERRORIST GROUPS THAT HAVE DISBANDED
BECAUSE THEY ACHIEVED THEIR OBJECTIVES

There are several notable examples of terrorist groups that have disbanded because they eventually assumed power and leadership of the states they fought to liberate. Some of these groups include the Irgun and Stern Gang during the British occupation of Palestine (1937–1948) and the National Liberation Front (FLN) in Algeria (1954–1962). These groups have few things in common other than being large and having widespread support, but they all achieved their goals.

Irgun

In 1937, a clandestine group of Jews who were opposed to the British occupation of Palestine began to attack British soldiers and Arabs. This group, known as Irgun Zvai Leumi, wanted to force the British to leave Palestine. It was also worried about Arabs present in so-called Jewish areas. The British government had placed restrictions on Jewish immigration to Palestine. From 1940 to 1943, while Great Britain fought in World War II, Irgun declared a truce with the British and supported Allied efforts to fight the Nazi regime in Germany.

As World War II was coming to a close, Irgun once again began its terror campaign, this time under the leadership of Menachem Begin, who later became the president of Israel. Because of an ideological squabble among Stern Gang members in 1940, a small faction broke away from Irgun. Shortly afterward, the group's leader, Avraham Stern, was assassinated by British troops, and that faction was reabsorbed into Irgun.[34] In February 1944, Irgun bombed the immigration department's offices in three of Palestine's major cities—Jerusalem, Tel Aviv, and Haifa—all at the same time. It also attacked the government land registry offices, the department of taxation and finance, and the security forces.[35] The group's biggest attack, however, was in July 1946 at the King David Hotel in Jerusalem. They set off a bomb that killed 91 people

Menachem Begin, center, speaks to supporters at his party's headquarters in Tel Aviv on May 18, 1977, as they celebrate the party's election to government. Begin, who was considered a terrorist during the movement for Israeli independence, was elected as the sixth prime minister of Israel.

and injured 41 others, including men, women, Arabs, Jews, and Britons.[36] The British public did not want its government to spend any more resources or be responsible for any more lost lives in what they perceived to be an untenable situation.

They were upset by incidents such as the King David Hotel bombing and the Irgun's July 1947 hanging of two British sergeants in response to the British government's execution of three convicted Irgun terrorists.[37] As a result, in September 1947, the colonial secretary announced that Britain would no longer govern Palestine, and all British nationals would be evacuated as soon as possible."[38]

On May 15, 1948, the United Nations partitioned Palestine into the modern Jewish state of Israel and the West Bank, primarily for Palestinians. Almost immediately, surrounding Arab states attacked Israel. The Irgun and Stern Gang attempted a power struggle with the sovereign state of Israel,

Menachem Begin (1913–1992)

Born in Brest-Litovsk, which is now part of Belarus, Begin became a leader of a local Zionist organization. Shortly thereafter, he was imprisoned by the Soviets before being released in 1941. He moved to Palestine (modern-day Israel) and soon joined the Irgun, a terrorist organization seeking the independence of Israel. Between 1945 and 1948, the Irgun committed several acts of terrorism in which British, Arab, and Jewish settlers died. One of the most famous of those attacks was the bombing of the King David Hotel, in which 91 people died, many of them British soldiers and officers. In 1947, Begin became Irgun's leader.

In 1948, when the British left Israel, the Irgun disbanded and Begin became the leader of the Herut, a conservative party. Later, in 1973, the Herut merged with other opposition parties to become the Likud. In 1977, Begin became the sixth prime minister of Israel. Two years later, under the leadership of U.S. President Jimmy Carter, Begin signed the Camp David Accords, a peace treaty with Egyptian president Anwar al-Sadat, and in 1978 they both received the Nobel Peace Prize. In 1982, however, Begin authorized the controversial invasion of Lebanon to route out Hezbollah and Palestinian terrorists, who were attacking Northern Israeli sites. Begin retired in 1983 and died in 1992.

A member of the national military organization Irgun Zvai Leumi looks for more ammunition during the 1947 armed Zionist revolt against the British rule of Palestine. After Israel gained independence in 1948, Irgun disbanded as its members joined the legitimate political process.

but they were declared a terrorist organization. Very quickly, most of the members disbanded and joined the legitimate political process.[39]

The National Liberation Front–Algeria (FLN)

After World War II, Algerians turned against their French colonial masters. The French and Muslim Algerians were antagonistic toward each other. Between 1954 and 1962, Algerians opposed to French authorities and colonial rule began an uprising that included numerous acts of terrorism. The French responded brutally to the insurgency and suspects. They drew inspiration and resources from similar efforts in the neighboring states of Tunisia and Morocco.

One of the turning points was the standoff popularly referred to as the Battle of Algiers (1954) and popularly presented in Gillo Pontecorvo's classic movie of the same title. In 1958, World War II hero Charles de Gaulle was chosen as president of France. He realized that the situation in Algeria was indefensible and supported Algeria's right to be its own country. At the same time, a secret organization of military officers, Secret Army Organization (OAS) formed in order to thwart de Gaulle's plans and even assassinate him. Its members planted bombs in Paris and Algiers and attacked Muslims in an effort to terrorize the population. In response to the FLN's activities and the growing French dissent, a cease-fire was declared in March 1962, and France began to pull its troops out of Algeria.[40]

TERRORIST ORGANIZATIONS THAT WERE DECIMATED PRIMARILY BECAUSE OF GOVERNMENT INTERVENTION

There are numerous examples of terrorist organizations that have been decimated (had their membership drastically reduced) by government actions. The organizations are divided among different ideological groups that have committed domestic and international terrorism in various countries. In order to organize this discussion, the various groups are listed under revolutionary/nationalist-separatist, left-wing, and right-wing divisions. With the exception of the Ku Klux Klan, many have been left-wing in nature.

Revolutionary/Nationalist-Separatist

A number of revolutionary/nationalist-separatist terrorist groups have been decimated by government intervention. Among those are include the Greek-Cypriot, Québécois, Armenian, and Puerto Rican groups.

The National Organization of Cypriot Fighters-Cyprus (EOKA)

In 1878, Great Britain took control of Cyprus, an island located in the Mediterranean. Approximately four-fifths of the island's inhabitants are primarily of Greek origin, and the balance are of Turkish roots. In 1955, EOKA—an organization led by retired Greek Army General George Grivas—proclaimed that it wanted to reunite the island with Greece. The British refused to leave: they wanted both to protect the Turkish minority and to use Cyprus as a strategic base. EOKA, however, took things into its own hands. The group stole explosives from the British army, smuggled weapons from Greece, bombed British government offices in Cyprus, and murdered British subjects and Cypriots. The attacks often took place in broad daylight and showed no mercy. Women, children, and members of the clergy were all murdered. Between 1954 and 1978, EOKA was responsible for 1,782 bombings and the deaths of 104 soldiers, 50 police officers, and 238 civilians. Meanwhile, 90 members of EOKA were killed during these violent activities. Several attempts were made to quell the conflict, including a partition between the Greek Cypriots and Turkish Cypriots. All parties eventually agreed to independence for Cyprus, however; the country was neither united with Greece nor partitioned. EOKA disbanded on December 31, 1958.[41]

Québécois Separatists

In Canada, the Front de Libération du Québéc (FLQ) operated from 1962 to 1972. It was primarily a nationalist-separatist organization, with left-wing sympathies. It wanted the predominantly French-speaking province of Quebec to break away from Canada and establish itself as a fully autonomous socialist state. This group was responsible for numerous bombings as well as the much-publicized 1970 kidnapping of British diplomat James Cross and the murder of Pierre Laporte a Canadian politician.[42]

Armenian Nationalist Terrorism

Armenian nationalists have directed their terrorism mainly against Turks. After multiple acts of genocide by Turks during World War I (during which about 1.5 million Armenians perished), several groups have tried to get even—primarily Armenians in the Baltic states and later in other places around the world. The attacks began in the 1890s, but this upsurge was short-lived. Armenian terrorists took further action in the 1890s and again after 1918, when they assassinated individual Turkish leaders who had been involved in the massacres. These kinds of activity have continued, on and off, until today. In 1975, there was an increase in Armenian terrorism.[43]

In January 1982, the Justice Commandos Against Armenian Genocide (JCAG)—a splinter group of the ASALA—assassinated the Turkish consulate general in Los Angeles. In May 1982, the honorary Turkish consulate general was assassinated in Boston. Later that year, the group's activities terminated with the arrest of its members, and Hampig Sassounian received a life sentence for committing the Los Angeles murder.[44]

Puerto Rican Terrorism

Puerto Rican terrorism can be traced back to 1868, when Puerto Rican nationalists engaged in violent actions in an attempt to gain independence from the United States or Spain. In general, the groups oppose what they perceive to be American imperialism. They want complete independence and share a Marxist-Leninist political ideology. Some observers and analysts believe that, since the 1960s, Puerto Rican terrorists have been supported by the Cuban government.[45]

Several terrorist incidents carried out by Puerto Rican groups have occurred in Puerto Rico and on the U.S. mainland, including the 1950 assassination attempt on former U.S. President Harry Truman and the 1954 shootings of five members of the U.S. House of Representatives.

Various Puerto Rican terrorist groups have emerged over the years to carry on the campaign, and there is solid evidence to indicate that some individuals belong to several different organizations. In the late 1960s, members of the Comandos Armados de Liberación (CAL) and Movimiento Independiente Revolucionario Armado (MIRA) claimed credit for numerous bombings in Puerto Rico and New York. Some attacks were aimed at U.S. companies that owned property on the island; others sought to discourage American tourism in Puerto Rico. Although the bombings stopped after a series of arrests, surviving members reorganized themselves as Fuerza Unida Revolucion Pro Independencia Armado (FURIA), which later reconstituted itself as the Fuerzas Armadas de Liberación Nacional (FALN).

FALN The FALN was one of the strongest and most active Puerto Rican terrorist organizations operating in the United States and, to a lesser extent, in Puerto Rico. The FALN was unknown to law enforcement until October 1975, when it claimed responsibility for five bombings in New York City. Over the next decade, this organization was credited with 72 actual bombings, 40 incendiary attacks, 8 attempted bombings, and 10 bomb threats; those incidents resulted in 5 deaths, 83 injuries, and more than $3 million in property damage.[46] In April 1980, 11 FALN members were arrested, including Carlos Torres, their leader at the time.

Lolita Lebron (center) and Andres Figueroa Cordero (in white shirt) are arrested by police officers in Washington, D.C., after they committed an attack on Capitol Hill, March 1, 1954. Lebron led a group of commandos in the attack, which was intended to bring attention to their struggle for a free Puerto Rico, independent of U.S. influence.

Macheteros–Ejército Popular Boricua On the island of Puerto Rico, the Ejército Popular Boricua (EPB) (more popularly known as the *Macheteros*, or the "machete-wielders") are both the most violent and the most effective of all the Puerto Rican terrorist groups. Formed in early 1970s, this group has been responsible for numerous murders and bank robberies. Several members of this group were arrested in 1985 and eventually put in jail. In August 1999, then-President Bill Clinton, in a controversial decision, granted clemency to 16 Puerto Rican terrorists from the FALN and the Macheteros.

Black Militant Terrorism

During the 1960s, there were numerous clashes between African Americans and the police—including controversial attempts by police to kill members of the Black Panthers in shootouts.[47] Few African American groups, such as the Black Panther Party (BPP), however, engaged in few incidents of domestic terrorism. For example, the Black Panther Party did not engage in political violence. One group that did pursue this strategy, however, was the Black Liberation Army. Formed as splinter group from the BPP between 1969 and 1973, the Black Liberation Army murdered police officers in New York City, Atlanta, Chicago, and San Francisco. In 1977, the Hanafi Muslim group, a militant Black Muslim organization, took over the headquarters of the B'nai B'rith in Washington, D.C.[48]

Hanafi Muslim Group

In 1977, about a dozen members of the Hanafi Muslim group, a militant Black Muslim organization, took over the district building (city hall), the B'nai B'rith, and the Islamic center building in Washington, D.C. A total of 134 individuals where held hostage at gunpoint for 39 hours. Marion Barry, then the mayor of Washington, was shot in the chest. Though he survived, a local radio reporter was killed. After the incident was resolved, those involved were handed down prison terms. Khalifa Hamaas Abdul Khaalis was sentenced to 21 to 120 years in jail.

Left-wing/Anarchist Groups

During the 1960s and 1970s, a considerable number of left-wing/anarchist terrorist groups existed, particularly in Western democracies. These groups included the Montoneros, Tupamaros, Japanese Red Army, Baader-Meinhof Gang/Red Army Faction, Direct Action (Action Directe), Weathermen/Weather Underground, Québécois Separatists, the Red Brigades, and Symbionese Liberation Army.

The Montoneros

The 1970s saw the formation of the Montoneros, a coalition of Catholic and left-wing groups in Argentina who opposed the pro-American regime and supported the exiled socialist leader Juan Peron. One of their earliest acts of terrorism was the kidnapping and killing of ex-president Pedro Aramburu. At their peak they could claim approximately 7,000 members. They supported themselves through very lucrative kidnappings of foreign executives and obtaining the ransom money. This group stepped up its terrorist attacks and criminal activities in 1975 and 1976, and this violent activity was partially responsible for ushering in a military dictatorship. Argentina was then subject to what was called the "Dirty War," during which close to 30,000 people died, 1,600 of which were Montoneros. The groups' activities started declining in 1977, although sporadic terrorist attacks continued into 1981. In 1983, military rule ended and democracy returned to Argentina; thus the need for the Montoneros was lessened.

The Tupamaros

In 1962, the Tupamaros formed in Uruguay and went on to bomb, kidnap, and assassinate military officers and other government officials. The group consisted of young professionals, such as teachers, lawyers, and doctors, and its activities led to the fall of the democratically elected government of Uruguay. The Tupamaros are best remembered for the 1970 murder of Dan Mitrione, an American advisor to the Uruguayan police force. By 1971, the Tupamaros held the all-time record for multiple and cumulative diplomatic highjackings. In response, the military seized power and used torture and other coercive means to destroy the Tupamaros. Most members of the Tupamaros fled into exile during this time period. In 1983, Uruguay's democracy was restored and new parliamentary elections were held. The Tupamaros reappeared as a peaceful political party and won a handful of seats in the new legislative body.[49]

Red Brigades

In 1969, the Red Brigades (also known as Brigate Rosse) formed in Italy. Documented in the movie *Year of the Gun*, its original members were drawn from the sociology department at the University of Trento. The group terrorized the judiciary, police, and big business and was responsible for the assassination of former premier and Christian Democratic Party leader Aldo Moro in 1978.[50]

The Japanese Red Army

At the same time, the Japanese Red Army (JRA) started in Japan. The group, which began operations in its home country, also then engaged in terrorism in various locations around the world. It was responsible for the Lod airport massacre (in Israel) in 1972 and it also carried out a number of spectacular highjackings.[51]

The Baader-Meinhoff Gang/Red Army Faction

The Baader-Meinhof Gang, which later reconstituted itself as the Red Army Faction (RAF), formed in 1977. This West German terrorist group was largely influenced by anarchist principles (decision making by consensus and against organized government). It was named after its two founders—Andreas Baader and Ulrike Meinhoff—and was responsible for bombing corporations and U.S. military installations, and for kidnapping German businessmen.[52]

Direct Action (Action Directe)

In 1979, the group Direct Action (Action Directe) formed in Belgium and France. It engaged in a widespread campaign of bombings and assassinations against government figures, Zionists, or businesses with Jewish connections. Later, the group was part of the European-wide, anti-NATO terrorist alliance that emerged in the 1980s.[53]

Summary

Most of the left-wing revolutionary groups present in North America, South America, and Western Europe no longer exist. The authorities defeated some of them. Others alienated their supporters with their choice of targets and tactics, and with their continuous doctrinal debates.[54]

Right-Wing Groups

Among the best-known right-wing terrorist groups that have disbanded because of government actions are the Ku Klux Klan, Anti-Castro Cubans, and various Italian groups.

The Klan

The Ku Klux Klan (KKK) was formed in the aftermath of the Civil War (1861–1865). Its organizational base consisted of white Southerners who were upset with the abolition of slavery and particularly with their own loss of status and power. They took their anger out on defenseless blacks through a ruthless campaign of terror that included cross-burnings, assaults, and lynchings. During its 150 years of existence, the KKK has gone through several different permutations as a result of internal competition and corruption.

In the 1960s and early 1970s, the Klan was involved in countless acts of intimidation or violence that were intended to intimidate and harass blacks and civil-rights workers. FBI investigations led to successful prosecutions in the federal courts, though, and, by the late 1960s and early 1970s, the Klan's terrorist activities had alienated many white Southerners.

In the 1980s, the Klan was primarily a loose collection of state-based organizations that were under the watchful eye of local law enforcement, the FBI, and several national watch-dog organizations, such as the Southern Poverty Law Center and the Anti-Defamation League. A number of lawsuits depleted the resources of these Klan-related organizations; thus, the frequency of their violent actions lessened. The KKK lives on, however, as does the attraction of some Americans toward racial and religious extremism.[55]

Italian Neo-Fascist Groups

Three main groups operated on the Italian right: the New Order, National Vanguard, and National Front. These groups, unlike most groups of the day, were radically opposed to Marxist-Leninist organization. Only in Italy did this kind of right-wing terrorism thrive.[56] After World War II, few neo-Fascist groups existed in Italy. The most prominent, the Italian Social Movement (MSI), formed in 1946. During the 1950s, disputes over doctrine resulted in the formation of a splinter group called the New Order. This new organization attacked left-wing organizations and targets in an effort to discredit them, and attempted to forge alliances with the national police, military, and other sympathetic groups throughout Europe.[57] Eventually, the New Order turned to terrorism and committed some of the more spectacular events in recent Italian history, including the now-famous bombing of the National Agricultural Bank at the Piazza Fontana in Milan (December 1969), in which 17 people were killed. The New

Order also claimed responsibility for the bombing of a train station in Bologna (August 1980), in which 84 people died and 180 were injured. The right was upset with the slow pace with which the government was dealing with the left-wing terrorists, and was also upset with the Communist and Socialist parties, who were considered to be too powerful.

Right-wing terrorism died out in Italy for three main reasons. First, new laws gave convicted terrorists longer sentences. Second, national security organizations were improved. Third, during the 1980s, Italy became less polarized.[58]

Anti-Castro Cubans

Cubans who were loyal to the former Batista regime or opposed to the Castro (Communist) government (1959–present) have carried out acts of violence against pro-communist entities in the United States and abroad (Canada). Four principal terrorist groups have been responsible for the violence: Alpha 66, El Poder Cubano, the Cuban National Liberation Front (FLN), and Omega 7. Many of these organizations have been supported by the United States government either materially, financially, or through training. It appears, however, that when these groups became more independent or hurt American citizens, the Central Intelligence Agency (CIA) stopped dealing with them.

The oldest Cuban anti-Castro group is Alpha 66; it is still led by members of the Cuban militia who participated in the ill-fated 1963 Bay of Pigs operation.[59] From 1968 to 1975, groups such as El Poder Cubano (Cuban Power) and the Cuban National Liberation Front were responsible for a series of bombings and assaults, and an assassination. From 1975 to 1983, a group called Omega 7 was the main source of Cuban émigré terrorism and posed a serious threat to the United States and Latin American countries that supported Fidel Castro. Seven key members of the group were arrested in 1982 and 1983, including Eduardo Arocena, the group's leader. Arocena was convicted and sentenced to life imprisonment." Shortly after his arrest, Omega 7 terrorism appeared to cease.[60]

TERRORIST ORGANIZATIONS THAT ENDED BECAUSE OF BURNOUT AND LACK OF SUPPORT

Some groups disbanded because members became frustrated with living underground, being constantly on the run, or

Significant Terrorist Groups That Have Disbanded or Been Decimated

At least 16 terrorist organizations are known to have disbanded. These include:

- Tupamaros, 1962–1978
- Québécois Separatists/Front de Liberation du Québéc, 1963–1972
- Red Brigades, 1969–approx. 1989/2003
- Japanese Red Army, 1971–1988
- Baader-Meinhof Gang/Red Army Faction, 1977–1998
- Weathermen/Weather Underground, 1969–approx. 1975
- United Freedom Front, 1976–1984
- Black Liberation Army, 1969–1973
- El Poder Cubano, 1968–1968
- Cuban National Liberation Front, 1972–1972
- Omega 7, 1975–1983
- Movimiento Independencia Revolucionario Armado (MIRA), 1967–early 1970s
- Fuerza Unida Revolutionaria Pro Independencia Armado (FURIA), 1974–1985
- Fuerzas Armadas de Liberación Nacional (FALN), 1975–1980
- Macheteros–Ejército Popular Boricua, 1970–1985

loss of support from their supporters. Such was true for the American based Weather Underground.

Weathermen/Weather Underground

Beginning in December 1969, the Weather Underground bombed government (including police and military) and corporate buildings, offices, and vehicles, starting in California and then moving to New York and other states. In September 1970, after allegedly being paid $20,000, they helped Timothy Leary (a psychologist and icon who advocated and popularized the use of the illegal drug LSD in the 1960s), escape from a prison in San Luis Obispo, California, and flee to Algeria.[61] By the late 1960s, the Weather Underground had acknowledged responsibility for at least 45 bombings throughout the country. In its first year, the group was credited with 500 bombings.[62]

On March 6, 1970, the New York cell was involved in the now-famous bomb explosion that went off prematurely, killing two members and damaging the group's Greenwich Village (New York) house. In 1971, the Weather Underground successfully placed a bomb in the U.S. Capitol, but it was discovered and safely defused. Also in 1971, the group planted a bomb at the California Department of Corrections building in San Francisco; this time the bomb exploded.

Although the group officially disbanded in the mid-1970s, many of its members were still in hiding or committing crimes periodically. The reasons behind the group's demise included the existence (and relative success) of more mainstream political groups like Vietnam Veterans Against the War, the debilitating effects of living on the run, and the final pullout of U. S. troops from Vietnam. The need for an antiwar movement had dissipated. The Weather Underground felt itself distanced from society; no one cared about its ideology anymore.

In the late 1970s, some of the remaining members who had been in hiding reconstituted themselves into a group called

M19CO. They allied themselves with members of the Black Liberation Army and individuals of a group called the Republic of New Africa. They were responsible for "liberating" a handful of so-called political prisoners from American jails and prisons.[63]

On October 20, 1981, members of M19C0 were involved in a $1.6 million Brinks truck robbery in Nyack, New York. This operation culminated in the shooting death of one Brinks employee and two police officers as well as the wounding of a security guard. Four individuals were eventually arrested, including former Weather Underground members Katherine Boudin and David Gilbert. Boudin and Gilbert have been in prison for the past 23 years and have been denied parole in connection with the robbery and shooting. By 2001, most of the other members of the Weather Underground had been arrested, were in prison, or had been released after serving jail sentences.

CONCEPTUAL ISSUES

Some analysts have suggested that there is a difference between antiterrorist and counterterrorist measures. The former are considered proactive (or offensive) actions designed to prevent terrorist incidents from happening (such as special legislation). The latter are thought of as reactive (or retaliatory) measures, usually through force, that a government takes after terrorism has occurred (such as air strikes or selective assassination).[64] Other observers and practitioners, however, have blurred the distinction and use these terms interchangeably.[65]

Another related distinction can be made between passive and active measures.[66] In general, passive responses attempt to prevent terrorist attacks. Tightened airport security is a response to hijacking and sabotage of aircraft; defensive steps labeled "target-hardening" are a response to bomb attacks; the "safety net" of individual security is a response to kidnapping.[67] Active approaches engage terrorists, in order to capture or kill them. Townsend notes, "The only chance of success in this direction lies in an effective intelligence system, using techniques such as infiltration and surveillance to acquire accurate information."[68]

In any security environment, tradeoffs must be made between the risk of attack, including its possible effects, and the cost of preventing the attack. Many security decisions are made in a political context, where reason is often subjugated in the name of expediency.[69]

CONCLUSION

It is clear that a considerable number of terrorist groups have disbanded because they achieved their objectives. Some gave up their use of violence because they formed a political party that gained a considerable amount of power. There were also a substantial number of organizations that were decimated or disbanded because of government actions.

CHAPTER 3

TERRORISM WILL CONTINUE:
GROUPS THAT STILL EXIST

INTRODUCTION

Many terrorist groups have long histories, despite setbacks and changes in leadership, internal dynamics, and membership. Some terrorist organizations show considerable endurance. They have been operating for a long time, replacing their losses, preparing for new attacks, and turning into semipermanent subcultures.

Most recent accounts put the number of active terrorist groups at 200. In 1991, terrorism expert Martha Crenshaw examined the longevity of 76 terrorist organizations. Many groups have exhibited remarkable stability and tenacity, but almost half either no longer exist or no longer commit acts of terror. At least ten groups, including Fatah, the Popular Front for the Liberation of Palestine-General

Command (PFLP-GC), and Euskadi Ta Askatasuna (ETA), however, have been in operation for at least 20 years.[70]

The group's longevity can be attributted to several factors. Generally speaking, the larger the group, and the more deeply held its grievances, the greater its chances for survival. Survival factors are intimately connected to the causes and effects of terrorism. In addition, certain kinds of terrorism simply seem to continue, such as those based on religious beliefs, and those connected to the cultivation and trafficking of narcotics (narcoterrorism).

GROUPS THAT HAVE CONTINUED TO COMMIT TERRORIST ACTS

Over the past four decades, several terrorist groups have changed their leadership, breadth, and number of members, but still advocate terrorism as part of their tactics. These organizations include the Aryan Nations, ETA, Fatah, the Provisional Irish Republican Army (PIRA), the Revolutionary Armed Forces of Colombia (FARC), and al Qaeda. In short, groups have transformed themselves superficially, but their grievances and ideologies have stayed the same.

The Aryan Nations, Splinter Groups, and Individuals

During the 1980s in the United States, acts of violent, right-wing terrorism were carried out by groups loosely affiliated with the Aryan Nations, including the Order, also known as the Covenant, the Sword, and the Arm of the Lord (CSA). Aryan Nations, which in its heyday had about 1,000 members, was based in the Pacific Northwest, particularly in Hayden Lakes, Idaho, (near Coeur d'Alene). It practiced or adhered to, as did many similar groups, "Christian Identity" beliefs.[71] The Aryan Nations established what appeared to be a survivalist training camp that became the home or stopping-over point for many individuals on the radical right (e.g., right-wing skinheads). At the Aryan Nations' compound, recruits would receive training in firearms and indoctrination in the group's philosophy and strategy. New members were recruited through word of mouth or through gun shows. In short, this group picked up where the Ku Klux Klan left off.

The Order (also known as the Bruder Schweigen, or Silent Brotherhood) was formed in 1983 by Robert Matthews and drew its inspiration from a book entitled *The Turner Diaries* (1978), written by William Pierce. Pierce's book was a blueprint designed to enable a band of right-wing sympathizers to overthrow the U.S. government.[72] The Order's members were responsible for many violent incidents, including bombings; assaults on federal officers; and the murder of a suspected informant, a Missouri state police officer, and Denver talkshow host Alan Berg.[73] To fund the organization, members of the Order committed a number of armed robberies and engaged in counterfeiting. From October 1984 to March 1986, 38 members of the Order were arrested. On December 7, 1984, Matthews was killed in a shootout with federal authorities on Whidbey Island, Washington (located in Puget Sound, just outside of Seattle).[74]

In the 1980s, the CSA committed bombings, arson, and robberies, and murdered a black Arkansas state police officer. In April 1985, federal authorities raided the CSA compound and arrested five people.[75]

In the mid-1980s, a number of groups loosely tied to the militia movement began to emerge. These included the Arizona Patriots and the White Patriot Party. In general, though, these groups lacked the organizational resources to carry out any significant terrorist activities.[76]

On April 19, 1995, Timothy McVeigh bombed the Alfred P. Murrah Federal Building in Oklahoma City. With the assistance of Terry Nichols (and, to a lesser extent, Michael Fortier), McVeigh—a decorated Gulf War veteran—parked a Ryder rental truck containing a powerful homemade bomb in front of the building. When the device exploded, it practically leveled the entire structure and caused considerable damage, injuries, and the deaths of 168 people. Although McVeigh had visited an Aryan Nations compound and claimed to be inspired by their ideology, most think that he was acting without the assistance of that organization.[77]

McVeigh and Nichols were apparently upset with the federal government's raid on the Branch Davidian compound in Waco, Texas (April 19, 1993), and the Alcohol, Tobacco, and Firearms (ATF)/Federal Bureau of Investigation's (FBI) assault on Randy Weaver's house in Ruby Ridge, Idaho (August 2, 1992).[78] In June 1997, McVeigh was convicted of conspiracy to blow up a government building. He was given the death penalty. Nichols was sentenced to life in prison, and Fortier received 12 years in a federal penitentiary. McVeigh was executed on June 11, 2001. Although some[79] point to a wider conspiracy among McViegh, Nichols, Fortier, and right-wing groups, federal authorities appear to have closed the book on this investigation.

Nevertheless, shortly after the Oklahoma City bombing, federal authorities began to crack down on the militia movement, some of which is loosely affiliated with right-wing terrorism. Of recent note, however, is the problem of the leaderless resistance, particularly among members of radical-right terrorist groups. Leaderless resistance is the process by which terrorist acts will be committed and terrorist organizations will exist without the benefit of a clearly identifiable key player.[80]

Euskadi Ta Askatasuna (ETA)

The Basques, who live in the northwestern part of Spain, have their own language and culture. Since the 1950s, Basques have struggled for independence from the rest of Spain. Those most committed to the struggle formed Euskadi Ta Askatasuna (ETA or "Basque Homeland and Security") in 1966 and by 1968 started terrorist activities. ETA-M, which describes itself as the military wing of the ETA, broke away from the main group in 1974. ETA-M was responsible for the worst atrocities of the 1970s and 1980s. Both groups, however, have waged a campaign

This photo shows people attending a meeting of the Euskal Herritarrok Party, considered to be a political arm of the ETA, in 2001. The Basque struggle for independence in Spain and France dates back to the 1950s.

under the name ETA. The campaign was most active between 1977 and 1980, but declined steadily throughout the 1980s. All together, ETA was responsible for more than 600 deaths between 1968 and 1996.[81] Some ETA members sought refuge in southern France. In the beginning, the French government accommodated them temporarily. In the 1980s, however, the French arrested and convicted about 80 Basques on terrorism-related charges.

Although most Basques are nationalistic and want more autonomy, they do not support terrorism. In response, the Spanish government has opened up the political system to the Basques, while allowing them to maintain their cultural heritage—a strategy that has served to defuse terrorism in Spain.[82]

Fatah

The Palestinian-Israeli conflict has spawned a number of terrorist organizations, including Fatah, the Popular Front for the Liberation of Palestine-General Command (PFLP–GC), the Democratic Front for the Liberation of Palestine (DFLP), the Abu Nidal Organization, and Hamas. One of the best-known and earliest established groups fighting for the creation of a separate homeland for the Palestinian people has been al Fatah (or Fatah, for short).

In 1957, Yasser Arafat and about 20 other individuals from different clandestine Palestinian groups formed Fatah in Kuwait.[83] They were influenced by the success of the Algerian revolution, in which nationalists, through an urban guerrilla campaign, successfully forced the French out of Algeria. Fatah has between 12,000 and 15,000 fighters and numerous support personnel.[84]

Over time, Fatah—also known as the National Palestine Liberation Movement—has become the "largest, oldest, and most influential Palestinian resistance organization."[85] Fatah disproportionately focuses on Palestinian nationalism. It does not support any particular political ideology or religious doctrine, despite the fact that many of its leaders are Muslims.[86]

In 1964, Arab nations established the Palestine Liberation Organization (PLO) as the governing body of the Palestinian people; Fatah quickly seized control. In June 1967, the neighbouring Arab countries of Egypt, Lebanon, Jordan, and Syria waged a combined military attack against Israel. Popularly known as the "Six-Day War," the Israelis not only thwarted the aggression, but also moved to occupy land in the four areas, including the Gaza Strip, Sinai Peninsula, Golan Heights, East Jerusalem, and the West Bank/Occupied Territories.

In September 1970, fearing a loss of political power, Jordan's King Hussein expelled high-ranking Palestinians living in his country. The majority relocated to southern Lebanon. Fatah then sought to gain a firm foothold in southern Lebanon, in order to gain a vantage point from which it could attack Israel. This involved Fatah in a Lebanese civil war, however, and led to the Israeli invasion of Lebanon in 1982. Fatah then began to struggle with other Arab regimes; one of the original reasons that Syria invaded Lebanon was to counter Arafat's influence.[87]

Shortly after the 1973 Yom Kippur War, (in which Egypt and Syria attempted to retake the land lost in the 1967 conflict), prominent Palestinian terrorist organizations lost hope in the Egyptians' and Syrians' ability to serve as benefactors. Fatah announced that it would cease engaging in international terrorist attacks (e.g., hijacking planes), which were proving to be less helpful to the cause than expected. Attacks taking place later were conducted by small, unauthorized factions.[88] The Palestinians' loss of hope was underlined when, in 1979, the governments of Israel and Egypt signed the Camp David Peace Accords. The PLO and, by extension, Fatah, recognized that they would have to deal with Israel directly and engage in some sort of compromise. In 1974, Arafat addressed the United Nations, which was a sign that he and his organizations were achieving international legitimacy.

In the mid-1970s, the Israelis (bolstered by United Nations forces) set up a security zone inside Lebanon, on its northern border. In June 1982, the Israelis, exhausted from cross-border attacks by Hezbollah and Palestinian factions, invaded Lebanon. Within days, Israeli tanks made their way to Beirut.[89] The United States brokered an agreement to have the Israelis and Palestinians leave, with American and French peacekeepers maintaining order. Palestinian fighters relocated to Algeria, Iraq, Tunisia, Yemen, and other Middle Eastern countries.[90]

In 1987, many Palestinian activists living in the occupied territories engaged in the Intifada, which primarily consisted of youths throwing rocks at the Israeli Army in the Gaza Strip and the West Bank. When the Israeli army overreacted by injuring and killing these youths, the world's media was present to broadcast the army shooting what appeared to be defenseless

From left: Egyptian President Anwar al Sadat, U.S. President Jimmy Carter, and Israeli Prime Minister Menachem Begin meet for the first time at Camp David on September 6, 1978. The following 12 days of secret negotiations resulted in the Camp David Peace Accords, which set the stage for future developments in the quest for peace in the Middle East.

youths. In the furor of the times, an Islamic fundamentalist group known as Hamas was born. Since that time, Hamas and Islamic Jihad have carried out numerous suicide attacks against the Israeli army and civilians inside the occupied territories and the state of Israel. These two splinter groups want to establish an Islamic state in these areas and do not recognize Israel's right to exist.[91] They are also seen as a threat to the leadership of the PLO.

In April 1993, the PLO and the Israeli government signed "The Declaration of Principles" (also known as the Oslo Accords), spelling out a number of agreements to work for peace between the two groups and the normalization of relations with the other Arab countries. Among the many concessions, Fatah would give up terrorism, and Israel would permit the Palestinians limited autonomy in the Gaza Strip and West Bank. Israeli Prime Minister Yitzhak Rabin and Palestinian leader Yasser Arafat were jointly awarded the Nobel Peace Prize for this accomplishment.

In 1994, the Palestinian National Authority (PNA) formed with the purpose of administering the Gaza Strip and West Bank. Arafat became the head of the PNA. Despite the accords, there is reason to believe that Fatah supports (financially and politically) armed factions or wings, such as Force 17, the Hawari Special Operations Group, Tanzim, and the al-Aqsa Martyrs' Brigade. In 2000, because of increased tensions between both parties, a second Intifada began. This movement was coupled with suicide bombings in crowded Israeli cities.

In the wake of 9/11, the United States has continued its efforts to broker a new peace agreement between Israel and the Palestinians. About a week after 9/11, U.S. President George W. Bush negotiated a cease-fire between Prime Minister Sharon and Yasser Arafat. If the cease-fire held for 48 hours, Foreign Minister Shimon Peres promised to reopen peace talks with Arafat, as well.[92]

In 2002, the Israeli Defense Forces have occupied the West Bank and surrounded Arafat's compound (located in Ramallah, West Bank), which was heavily affected by shelling. Several assassinations and assassination attempts have been carried out against the leadership of Al-Aqsa Martyrs' Brigade and Hamas. Meanwhile, suicide bombings take place on a weekly basis inside Israel.

On November 11, 2004—two weeks after Arafat was transported to a hospital in France for treatment of an intestinal disorder—he slipped into a coma and died. Many international leaders are hoping that Arafat's death will pave the way to increased peace in the Israeli–Palestinian conflict. Nonetheless, Fatah and its splinter groups are a classic example of a long-surviving terrorist group.

Revolutionary Armed Forces of Colombia (FARC)

Three so-called narcoterrorist groups operate in Colombia: the United Self-Defense Forces of Colombia (AUC), the National Liberation Army (ELN), and the Armed Forces of Colombia known as Fuerzas Armadas Revolucionarias de Colombia (FARC). The FARC is the largest, best-trained, and most deadly of the three.

The FARC is an extreme, left-wing, communist-inspired organization with a reported membership of 12,000 to 18,000.[93] Established in 1964, this group is led by the aging Manuel Marulanda and six others, including senior military commander Jorge Briceno. Although its origins are murky, the group first came to public attention in 1966 as the military wing of the Colombian Communist Party.[94]

Part of the reason for the FARC's success is its ability to develop a loyal following among Colombia's poor, especially the peasants and the indigenous people who live in relatively remote rural areas. This group has accumulated significant resources through the drug trade (specifically, coca, opium/poppy, and marijuana), either through cultivation or by providing security for traffickers.[95]

The primary objective of the FARC is to overthrow the Colombian government. Other demands include increased political equality, a reduction in unemployment, an end to privatization of industry, and a redistribution of wealth. FARC is anti-American; it believes that the United States is an imperialist country, especially because of its intervention in Colombian affairs. Ironically, the group believes that Colombia should legalize drugs. This, they say, would reduce the violence and negative effects of illegal drugs. Because of its connection to drug trafficking, the FARC maintains links to criminal gangs in Ecuador, Panama, and Venezuela.

The FARC engages in kidnappings, bank robberies, and drug trafficking in order to finance the organization. It has been responsible for assassinations, kidnappings, car bombings, and the hijacking of an airliner. It targets government, military, locally elected municipal mayors, police, and civilians. Most of its attacks have been confined to Colombia. Rarely has FARC engaged in terrorism outside of that country.

In the later 1980s, the FARC established the Patriotic Union (UP), a political party, but the UP fell victim to right-wing death squads sponsored by drug lords and the Colombian military. An estimated 3,000 UP members were killed, including its 1990 presidential candidate Bernardo Jaramillo Ossa.[96]

In 1998, Colombian President Pastrana granted the FARC a 16,216-square-mile (42,000-square-kilometer) safe haven as a concession to sit down to peace talks. In 2001, Pastrana once again began talks with FARC about a peace treaty. Negotiations dragged on, though, and Pastrana threatened to end the demilitarized zone (an area about the size of Switzerland).[97] The peace process with the government continued at a slow pace for three years, during which time news organizations discovered that the group was recruiting children as soldiers, importing arms, exporting drugs, and building up its military capabilities. After the FARC allegedly kidnapped a Colombian presidential candidate, Ingrid Betancourt, and other political figures, Pastrana ended the peace talks in February 2002 and ordered the Colombian military to retake the FARC-controlled area.[98]

Since the 9/11 attacks, the U.S. government has given the Colombian government $3 billion to combat the FARC. Operation Black Cat, which commenced in February 2002, was a military offensive directed against the FARC, with the use of aircraft and helicopters. At the same time, Pastrana annulled the FARC's political status and issued arrest warrants for its leaders. In the February 12 attack, the Colombian military struck so far into FARC territory that the FARC was taken totally by surprise.[99]

The FARC's attacks on the Colombian government have led to the development of death squads. These are paramilitary organizations that torture actual or suspected members of

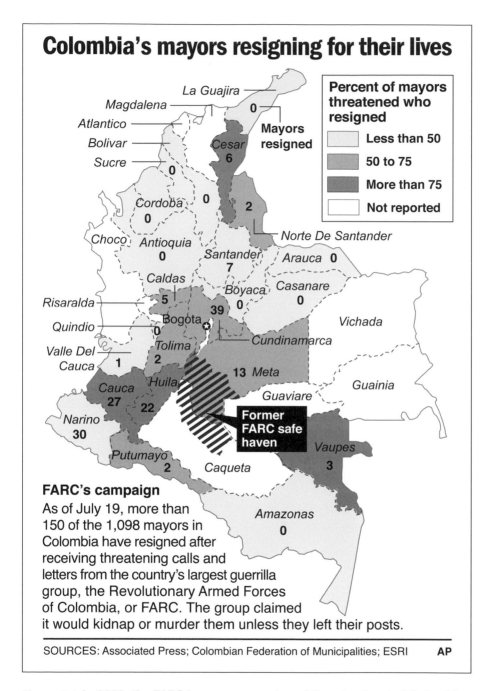

Colombia's mayors resigning for their lives

La Guajira
Magdalena
Atlantico
Bolivar
Sucre

Percent of mayors threatened who resigned

	Less than 50
	50 to 75
	More than 75
	Not reported

Mayors resigned

Cesar
6

La Guajira
0

Cordoba
0

0

2

Norte De Santander

Choco   Antioquia
0

Santander
7

Arauca 0

Caldas

Boyaca Casanare

Risaralda
5

39

0

0

Vichada

Quindio
Bogota
0

Cundinamarca

Valle Del
Cauca
1

Tolima
2

13 Meta

Guainia

Cauca
27

Huila

22

Guaviare

Narino
30

Former FARC safe haven

Vaupes
3

Putumayo
2

Caqueta

FARC's campaign

As of July 19, more than 150 of the 1,098 mayors in Colombia have resigned after receiving threatening calls and letters from the country's largest guerrilla group, the Revolutionary Armed Forces of Colombia, or FARC. The group claimed it would kidnap or murder them unless they left their posts.

Amazonas
0

SOURCES: Associated Press; Colombian Federation of Municipalities; ESRI   AP

Figure 3.1 **In 2002, the FARC began a campaign of threats aimed at Colombian mayors, with the intent of forcing many to resign. This graphic shows what percentage of threatened mayors resigned in each region of the country.**

terrorist organizations or their sympathizers and engage in extra-judicial killings and "disappearances."

From 2002 to 2004, the FARC was thought to be retreating because of the increasing military and police actions of the new hardline president, Alvaro Uribe Velez. Velez's tough stance has led to the capture or desertion of many fighters and medium-level commanders. The most important event happened in January 2004, when police captured Simon Trinidad, a former banker turned rebel, who had participated as a high-profile negotiator in the recent Pastrana peace talks.[100]

During its 40 years of existence, the FARC has also developed enemies beyond the national government, including the National Liberation Army (ELN), the smaller of the two main Marxist terrorist organizations in Colombia. The FARC apparently has very little international support and must rely on its own businesses, yet it continues to exist and even prosper.[101]

Provisional Irish Republican Army (PIRA)

The IRA struggle is centuries old.[102] In order to understand this conflict, one needs to be familiar with the history, politics, and economy of Ireland. Among other notable features of this conflict is Irish Catholics' desire for autonomy from British rule, which has waxed and waned under a variety of circumstances. At certain points in history, the struggle has had a religious basis; at other times, it has been the result of grievances that are simply economic and political (such as the subjugation of Catholics to British, and therefore Protestant, rule). Some analysts have suggested that the conflict has ethnic rather then religious roots.[103]

A few highlights may help to clarify this conflict. After a popular rebellion led by Michael Collins and others, the Irish Free State (now known as the Republic of Ireland) was established in 1921, encompassing 26 of 32 counties; the remaining 6 northern counties came under British protection and are generally called Northern Ireland. In Northern Ireland (popularly referred to as Ulster), from the time of the split until the mid 1960s, the civil rights of Catholics living in the north decreased.[104] Catholics disproportionately held the least desirable jobs and occupied inferior housing and education, affecting their ability to get ahead socially and economically. Since 1968, almost 3,600 individuals have died in this conflict. The dead include not only British military but also police officers and innocent civilians.

During the 1960s, partially inspired by the civil rights movement in the United States, Protestants and Catholics began to demand improved housing conditions and educational opportunities. The repression by the Northern Irish government made things worse, however. According to White,

> Catholics were not allowed to demonstrate . . . ; if they attempted to do so, they were attacked by the RUC [Royal Ulster Constabulary—the local police force] and its reserve force known as the B-Specials. At the same time no attempts were made to stop Protestant demonstrations. The Catholics believed the RUC and B-Specials were in league with the other anti-Catholic unionists in the North.[105]

Catholics and Protestants who were pro-unionist/republicans were essentially at each others' throats.[106]

In August 1969, riots erupted in Belfast and Londonderry. Local police were relatively ineffective against this kind of civil disturbance. As a result, the British government increased the number of soldiers stationed there. The army—interpreting the situation as a colonial war—quickly allied itself with the Protestants. This only served to polarize the Catholics and Protestants further. The British military also uncritically allied itself with the Royal Ulster Constabulary (RUC). The army would surround Catholic neighborhoods, break down doors, and throw tear gas and smoke bombs—all in an effort to draw out terrorists and their sympathizers. The Catholics wanted the army out, and many Protestants believed that they could act with impunity against Catholics.[107]

As a result of this sectarian violence, the Irish Republican Army (IRA) reconstituted itself and started engaging in terrorist actions. In December 1969, the IRA split into the "Officials" and the "Provisionals." This created unnecessary confusion among outsiders, as both organizations had military and political wings.[108] In the summer of 1972 the "Official" IRA declared a ceasefire. It put its energy into supporting Sinn Fein, the political party established to seek independence for Northern Ireland from Great Britain. Members who were unhappy with this shift to mainstream politics formed a breakaway group called the "Provisional IRA." Since that time, the term *IRA* has often been used to refer to the organization that had developed from the "Provisional IRA."[109] Membership in the IRA increased to between 1,500 and 2,000 members during the 1970s, and dropped to about 300 to 500 members after the 1994 ceasefire was signed.[110]

In 1973, the British government passed the Northern Ireland (Emergency Provisions) Act, which allowed the military greater powers of search and detention of terrorist suspects. The army could enter anyone's house at any time, without obtaining a warrant. During the same year, the IRA launched a campaign of bombings on the British mainland in cities, including London. Meanwhile, the level of violence in Northern Ireland has intensified in cycles, including 1972, 1974, the early 1980s, the late 1980s, and the early 1990s.[111] Loyalists engaged in considerable violence, attacking the RUC and the army, and assassinating Republican leaders. The IRA eventually concentrated primarily on the British state's representatives, the RUC, the army, unionist and British politicians, and the British Royal Family. By the early 1990s, though, IRA members and loyalists had become engaged in a mounting series of revenge-type murders.[112]

Sinn Fein president Gerry Adams (bottom center) attends an IRA commemoration in Northern Ireland, Sunday, February 20, 2005. Adams, a member of the IRA since 1964, has been an important part of the Northern Ireland peace process.

Several positive steps have occurred in the long-standing conflict.[113] In 1985, the United Kingdom and the Republic of Ireland signed a peace accord regarding the governance of Northern Ireland. Known as the Anglo-Irish Peace Accord, the agreement was intended to bring terrorism to an end by establishing a joint system of government in the troubled area.[114] In 1998, the IRA signed a peace agreement with Great Britain, which is popularly known as The Good Friday (or Belfast) Agreement. In 1999, a power-sharing agreement was started in the Northern Ireland Assembly. In 2001, the IRA began to give up its weapons, and, in 2002, Martin McGuiness and Gerry

Gerry Adams (1949–)

Born in West Belfast, Gerard Adams, Jr., joined Sinn Fein, generally considered to be the political wing of the Irish Republican Army (IRA), in 1964. Although both groups claim that they are entirely separate, and Adams denies being a member of the IRA, the British government and press have labeled him as such. Since 1971, under the controversial Special Powers Act, he has repeatedly been in and out of British prisons. He was released to take part in the 1972 peace talks, but returned to prison from 1973 to 1977. In 1978, he became vice president of Sinn Fein.

In 1983, Sinn Fein experienced a major split over strategy between a southern wing, later calling itself the Republican Sinn Fein, and a northern wing, under the direction of Adams. This split facilitated Adams's rise to be the leader of Sinn Fein. During this time, Adams, together with other members of Sinn Fein, won seats in the British House of Commons. In 1984, Adams was wounded during an assassination attempt. Although at first Sinn Fein did not want to recognize the authority of the British state or that of the Republic of Ireland, to the south, its leaders slowly and secretly started working toward a peace accord, later dubbed the Belfast Agreement or Good Friday Agreement with Great Britain, and an IRA cease-fire began in 1994.

Adams (IRA leaders and representatives) received offices in the British Parliament, but refused to take seats—this would mean they would need to sign an oath to the Queen of England, something they virulently opposed.

Al Qaeda

Osama bin Laden and his organization, al Qaeda, aided the rise of the Taliban (the former leadership of Afghanistan). Since the Soviet pullout from Afghanistan in February 1989, al Qaeda has sponsored a number of anti-American attacks.[115] Although countless histories of al Qaeda, the Taliban, and the Soviet invasion and occupation of Afghanistan exist, for our purposes, the history can be summarized as follows: In 1979, the Soviet Union invaded Afghanistan. Meanwhile, a considerable number of Afghan Arabs, as they were called, were emboldened by their success and sought additional international targets. One source claims the number of Afghan Arabs is close to 17,000, whereas the British *Janes Intelligence Review* puts the number at about 14,000 (about 5,000 Saudis, 3,000 Yemenis, 2,000 Egyptians, 2,800 Algerians, 400 Tunisians, 370 Iraqis, 200 Libyans, and a number of Jordanians.[116] Two of those men were Ramzi Yousef and Osama bin Laden.

PROBLEMS IN COMBATTING TERRORISM

The reactions to terrorism in general, and to counterterrorism in particular, involves a whole host of political actors (e.g., policymakers, practitioners, and citizens), with competing resources, agendas, and interests. Interpreting and balancing what these groups want and need is no easy task. Part of the issue is whether government agencies should, or must, adhere to the rule of law, or—given the unusual nature of terrorism—can circumvent state-based constitutions and internationally mandated human rights documents and practices by responding with extraordinary force.[117] The dilemma is not easily resolved in a manner that satisfies all parties involved.

Over the past four decades, the methods by which countries combat terrorism has changed. With each rash of incidents, new countermeasures are implemented. It is then only a matter of time before terrorist organizations find new weaknesses to exploit.

Governments have countered terrorism in eight different ways, including (from least to most important or most frequently used):

1. Development of databases and collection of relevant intelligence;

2. Creation and use of "third forces," special military units, or SWAT teams to handle terrorist situations;

3. Development and use of antiterrorist technology;

4. Signing and implementation of new treaties among countries;

5. Signing and enforcement of new laws against national and international terrorism;

6. Increased use of intelligence; and

7. More surveillance of suspected terrorists and their supporters;

8. Hardening of actual and potential targets.

Nevertheless, some of the difficulties that stand in the way of effectively countering terrorism include the lack of a definition of the term *terrorism* that is commonly accepted by government agencies, plus a lack of cooperation—not only among state agencies who have an interest in monitoring terrorism, but also among countries that may have helpful intelligence. Most of these entities are reluctant to share information, especially intelligence, unless they believe that it is in their short-term political interests.

Countries and their national security agencies must also carefully balance citizens' individual freedoms against the pursuit of terrorists. Otherwise, there would be too much repression, and the legitimacy of the existing regime will be called into question. In reprisals for terrorist actions, there is always the possibility of collateral damage, especially when innocent civilians are detained, injured, or killed, or when property is damaged or destroyed.[118] This outcome is an all-too-familiar consequence of America's involvement in Afghanistan and Iraq.

Finally, the issue of measuring the effectiveness of combating terrorism is a thorny one. According to Townsend, "If we look for precise evaluation of the effectiveness of antiterrorist policies we find it is surprisingly thin on the ground. Very few indeed of the many writers on terrorism have produced a statistical analysis of key countermeasures."[119] Policymakers and practitioners would be well advised to keep these factors in mind when they comment on or propose and implement measures designed to combat terrorism.

THE POWERFUL EFFECTS OF RELIGIOUS FUNDAMENTALISM AND NARCOTERRORISM

Religious Fundamentalism

By the mid-1980s, a number of Islamic fundamentalist and Middle Eastern terrorist groups formed. Three of the most prominent Islamic fundamentalist groups are Hezbollah, Islamic Jihad, and Hamas. In addition to their fiery rhetoric, they have carried out numerous suicide bombings. Such bombings usually involve a car or truck, laden with explosives, driven into a military vehicle, barracks, or compound. Alternatively, an individual carrying explosives concealed on his or her body may walk into a crowded market or bus station. When the bomb explodes, not only will it kill the driver or courier, but it will also cause considerable injuries and death among citizens and soldiers who are present.

President Clinton, with Israeli prime minister Yitzhak Rabin (left) and PLO chairman Yasir Arafat (right), presides over ceremonies marking the signing of the 1993 peace accord between Israel and the Palestinians. Although the accord was heralded as a major step toward peace, the struggle between the two parties has continued and even escalated in recent years.

Hezbollah, which means Party of God, emerged in Lebanon during the 1980s. Originally, it was established with help from Iran to remove the Israelis from Palestine, but it now aids the Palestinians in their historical struggle against Israel. Motivated by the success of the Iranian Revolution, this group originally wanted to establish a theocratic state in Lebanon; it has since abandoned this approach and now has elected members who serve in the Lebanese parliament. It gained international prominence through a series of high-profile kidnappings of prominent Americans and was also responsible for the 1983 suicide bombing of the U.S. Marine barracks in Beirut. Its numbers are counted in the thousands.[120]

The Islamic Jihad, another Shiite fundamentalist organization, is based in Damascus and has financial support from Syria and Iran. It has concentrated its suicide bombings in Israel against soldiers and civilians. It wants to create an Islamic Palestinian state and is against pro-Western Arab states. It has staged attacks in Jordan and Lebanon, two of the most Western-friendly of the Arab states.[121]

Started in 1987 after the Intifada, Hamas does not recognize Israel's right to exist and wants Palestinians to have the right to rule the land granted to the Israelis before the 1949 mandate. Although the actual number of Hamas members is unknown, it has thousands of supporters as well as military and political wings. It has been responsible for several suicide bombings targeting Israeli citizens. Hamas has also been antagonistic to the Palestinian National Authority, leading to the 1996 PNA arrests of 1,000 Hamas members. Its base of support is primarily in Gaza and it has operated at times with the assistance of the Jordanian government.[122] In January 2006, Hamas won the legislative election and at the time of this writing is forming a parliament.

Narcoterrorism

In the early 1990s, the terms *narcoterrorism* and *gray area phenomenon* were introduced into the terrorism lexicon. The first term refers to the "use of drug trafficking to advance the objectives of certain governments and terrorist organizations"—identified as the Marxist-Leninist regimes of the Soviet Union, Cuba, Bulgaria, and Nicaragua, among others.[123] Powerful cultivators of illegal drugs and traffickers formed alliances with terrorist groups for mutual benefit. Among regions that have generated interest in the narcoterrorism phenomenon are the Middle East, Africa, and Asia—all containing countries that are major cultivators, distributors, and processors of drugs. The majority of interest has focused on Latin America—Colombia in particular, however, where the cocaine cartel needed protection, and rebel forces wanted resources (primarily money). This relationship combined the essential elements of not only terrorism, but also organized crime and state sponsorship, especially when the state, and those in positions of power, were corrupt. In these contexts, ideological concerns were placed on hold and access to money prevailed.[124]

Much of the narcoterrorist activity in Colombia has centered on Medellin, the epicenter of cocaine trafficking and the alleged home of the drug cartel. Car bombs explode and people are kidnapped or assassinated there on a routine basis in response to the government's antidrug campaign. In August 1989, stories emerged about British and Israeli mercenaries who were training and advising the Colombian drug lords and gangs.[125] Some say that the mercenaries were used to combat communist guerillas. Apparently Pablo Escobar, the cartel's leader, allied himself with the April 19 Movement (M-19) and with the Revolutionary Armed Forces of Colombia (FARC).

CONCLUSION

This chapter has placed into context the different terrorist groups that have, despite government efforts, persisted for a number of decades. They have numerous sympathizers in the general population and have occasionally fielded political candidates in order to participate in traditional politics in the countries in which they live.

CHAPTER 4

TERRORISM IS CYCLICAL

INTRODUCTION

When thinking about terrorism, we tend to get caught up in the immediate horror of terrorist events, while ignoring long-term patterns. In order to have a better understanding of the patterns of contemporary terrorism, the following section provides a description of a number of trends—including the frequency of terrorist incidents, geographic spread, targets, tactics, and terrorist groups.

CONTEMPORARY TRENDS

By reviewing acts of terrorism that have occurred over the past 37 years, one can see the ebb and flow in terms of the number of events, geographic spread, targets, and tactics used. The statistics of

International Terrorist Incidents: 1968–June 30, 2005*

YEAR	NUMBER OF INCIDENTS
1968	106
1969	103
1970	180
1971	157
1972	210
1973	175
1974	237
1975	213
1976	330
1977	240
1978	224
1979	227
1980	240
1981	305
1982	366
1983	287
1984	328
1985	440
1986	378
1987	364
1988	375
1989	362
1990	286
1991	421
1992	273
1993	273
1994	312
1995	267
1996	240
1997	171
1998	161
1999	125
2000	103
2001	205
2002	297
2003	274
2004	330
2005	134

*Data from MIPT Terrorism Knowledge Base, www.tkb.org.

Figure 4.1 **This chart sums up the number of terrorist incidents that occurred internationally each year from 1968 to 2005.**

terrorism, however, are a bit difficult to verify. There are many different databases that record such statistics—the most widely used of which was, until recently, a joint venture between the U.S. State Department and the CIA.[126] Like other databases (some of which are run by organizations, while others are maintained by individuals), the U.S. State Department database contains inaccuracies due to a number of factors. Issues that arise include data limited to certain years; data that includes hoaxes and threats that never came to fruition; and limited geographical scope. In addition, in April 2005 the State Department formally announced that it would no longer make global reports on terrorism.[127] Instead, this function would be handed over to the National Counterterrorism Center, which is part of the Central Intelligence Agency (CIA). Because of these recognized issues, the information in this chapter is based on a variety of sources, including information from the State Department's "Patterns of Global Terrorism" reports, RAND reports, or MIPT (terrorism knowledge base-tkb) data. It is important to note that that data for 1968–1997 covers only international incidents, whereas the statistics for 1998 through June 30, 2004, cover domestic and international incidents.

The majority of the available data on terrorism shows the same general pattern, despite the drawbacks related to each data set. As a reminder, this data reflects only incidents of international terrorism.[128]

Many acts of terrorism are successfully thwarted by the combined efforts of law enforcement and national security agencies. Due to fears that sensitive information connected to ongoing investigations will be leaked or will impact the likelihood of a conviction when the case comes to trial, rarely are these successes made public.[129] This information should help us better understand the data. In other words, the available databases may underestimate the actual terrorism that is perpetrated or is in the process of being organized.

Annual Statistics

From 1968 to June 30, 2005, there were approximately 9,718 international political terrorist events, ranging from a low of 103 incidents in 1969 and 2000 to a high of 440 in 1985. This breaks down to an average of about 259 incidents each year.[130] The prevailing impression given by the media, public officials, and some experts concerned with international terrorism, however, is that terrorism is on the increase. For the most part, increases are relative to the time period under investigation; terror attacks are not linear, as media accounts might imply. As far back as the 1960s, the frequency of terrorism has been cyclical, with several peaks and valleys. This is not surprising, as general factors cause increases and declines, as shall be demonstrated. In 2004, the most recent complete year for which statistics are available, the total number of international terrorist incidents was 330—that is 56 events more than occurred in 2003. Not all events were of the same magnitude and intensity, however. For example, the magnitude of the September 11, 2001, attacks on the World Trade Center and the Pentagon might lead to the conclusion that there has been a steep increase in the number of terrorist events overall, which is not actually the case.

Geographic Spread

The number of countries experiencing some sort of terrorist activity each year has gradually increased. In the late 1960s, international terrorist incidents occurred in an average of 29 countries each year. This average climbed to 39 countries in the early 1970s and 43 countries in the late 1970s. For the first three years of the 1980s, the average number of countries experiencing international terrorist incidents was 51; for the period from 1983 to 1985, the average was 65 incidents.[131]

Although terrorism takes place throughout the world, some regions currently suffer a disproportionate amount of the world's terrorism. Regions experiencing the largest number of terrorist activities change almost every year. Between 1968 and June 30, 2005, for example, the Middle East received the brunt of terrorist attacks (6,743), while East and Central Asia incurred the lowest number of incidents (198).[132] About 20 countries account for between 75 and 90 percent of all reported incidents. The top three countries that experience the largest amount of terrorism (approximately 75 percent) are, in descending order of frequency, Israel (including the Gaza Strip and the West Bank), Pakistan, and Colombia.

Databases on Oppositional Political Terrorism

When a data source on terrorism is cited, it is commonly either the Control Risks Group database, RAND Corporation database, or the State Department/Central Intelligence Agency/International Terrorism: Attributes of Terrorist Events (ITERATE) I, II, and III data sets.

First, the London-based Control Risks Group (http://www.crg.com) maintains a data set on domestic and international terrorism. Formed in 1975, this business (with more than 400 employees and 16 offices worldwide) serves the security requests of businesses and corporations. The company specializes in the following four areas: "political and security risk analysis," "confidential investigations," "security responses," and "crisis response." Not only do its country files contain data on terrorist actions, but they also include information on criminal behavior. Updated monthly, the "Data Solve" information system from Control Risks Information Services is available in several formats.

Second, the RAND Corporation (http://www.rand.org), headquartered in Santa Monica, California, is an independent, "nonprofit" think tank that performs contract- and grant-funded research for various sponsors, mainly the government and large businesses. It has gained a reputation for conducting wide-ranging studies on subnational, low-intensity conflict and domestic and international

Targets

Since the 1960s, the range of terrorist targets has expanded. At the beginning of the 1970s, terrorists concentrated their attacks mainly on property and institutions; in the 1980s, they increasingly targeted people. Almost every conceivable structure has been hit, including embassies, factories, airliners, airline offices, tourist agencies, hotels, airports, bridges, trains, train stations, reactors, refineries, schools, restaurants, pubs, churches, temples, synagogues, mainframe computers for large businesses and organizations, data-processing centers, and office towers.

terrorism. It has also constructed a number of databases on various topics pertaining to terrorism. Although RAND's data sets are not available for public analysis, some of the reports generated with these data make it into the public domain.

Finally, the State Department/CIA/ITERATE (http://www.state.gov) data sets have become the best known and most widely used public sources for researchers studying international terrorism. Roughly 150 variables per case are coded. Originally, this database was developed from two RAND chronologies and from press accounts in the *New York Times*, the *Washington Post*, and other prominent media sources. By 1980, it listed more than 200 sources. ITERATE has three major advantages: (a) It is publicly available for a nominal cost. (b) ITERATE I and II are accessible for free from member institutions of the Inter-university Consortium of Political and Social Research, located at the University of Michigan. (c) It has a readily accessible chronology and a code book, so researchers can use it to check the validity of coding or create their own data sets. On the downside, however, the State Department data set is limited to international terrorism, and data for most charts is limited to the years between 1981 and the present.

Terrorist Incidents by Region, January 1, 1968 to July 30, 2005

REGION	INCIDENTS	INJURIES	FATALITIES
Africa	989	8,742	3,352
East & Central Asia	198	5,344	223
Eastern Europe	1,215	4,901	1,873
Latin America	3,398	3,514	2,175
Middle East / Persian Gulf	6,743	24,468	9,840
North America	582	1,845	3,574
South Asia	3,349	17,374	5,968
Southeast Asia & Oceania	736	3,685	1,248
Western Europe	5,244	5,372	1,389

Figure 4.2 **This table breaks down the total number of incidents from 1968 to 2005, based on region of the world. It also indicates how many injuries and fatalities were suffered in each region as a result of the attacks.**

A considerable amount of public and media attention has been directed toward the possibility of terrorist attacks on nuclear facilities and the potential of resulting radioactive fall-out. Indeed, there have been breaches of security at these places; most of the incidents, however, were carried out by antinuclear protestors trying to halt or delay the construction of new nuclear facilities, not terrorists trying to destroy existing facilities.

Americans, the British, the French, Israelis, and Turks account for approximately half of all the nationalities victimized by terrorists.[133] The individuals attacked include diplomats, military personnel, tourists, businesspeople, students, journalists,

Total Terrorist Events by Target, January 1, 1968–July 30, 2005

TARGET	INCIDENTS	INJURIES	FATALITIES
Abortion Related	5	2	2
Airports & Airlines	805	2,375	2,359
Business	3,258	9,734	4,933
Diplomatic	2,620	8,413	1,273
Educational Institutions	416	1,349	475
Food or Water Supply	9	5	0
Government	3,312	7,301	3,456
Journalists & Media	483	221	181
Maritime	134	263	130
Military	798	4,362	1,450
Non-Governmental Organizations	286	256	264
Other	1,446	2,181	1,450
Police	1457	4,963	2,822
Private Citizens & Property	3,831	13,885	5,714
Religious Figures/Institutions	762	4,927	1,662
Telecommunication	121	73	35
Terrorists	216	513	402
Tourists	244	1,495	585
Transportation	896	11,688	1,936
Unknown	659	903	317
Utilities	699	336	196
TOTAL	22,457	75,245	29,642

Figure 4.3 This table shows a breakdown of the total number of terrorist incidents (1968–2005), based on the targeted organizations, individuals, or institutions.

children, nuns, priests, and the pope. According to MIPT/tkb statistics, since 1968, the majority of targets have been private citizens and property (3,821).

From 1968 to June 30, 2005, of the 22,457 incidents, there were a total of 75,245 injuries and 29,642 fatalities.[134] Based on 2004 State Department figures, about 16 percent (2,998 individuals) were American citizens.

By the end of 2001, largely because of the events of 9/11, the number of deaths rose to approximately 3,000. Typically, only 15 to 20 percent of all terrorist incidents involve fatalities; of those, 66 percent involve only one death. Less than one percent of the thousands of terrorist incidents that have occurred in the past two decades involve ten or more fatalities. Incidents of mass murder, sometimes achieved through suicide bombings, are truly rare. This has led some experts, like Brian Jenkins, to repeatedly suggest that "terrorists want a lot of people watching rather than a lot of people dead."[135]

TACTICS

Terrorists operate with a fairly limited repertoire of attacks. Seven basic tactics have accounted for 97 percent of all terrorist incidents: bombings (13,217), assassinations (2,182), armed assaults (3,657), kidnappings (1,652), arson (868), hijackings (232), and barricade and hostage incidents (201).[136] In short, terrorists blow things up, kill people, or seize hostages. Every incident is essentially a variation on these activities. Bombings appear to be the most deadly.

Although the use of weapons of mass destruction (WMD), such as biological, chemical, nuclear, or toxic weapons is a topic of constant concern, bombings of all types continue to be the most popular terrorist method of attack. Approximately 50 percent of all international events are bombings. This is followed, in terms of numbers, by armed attacks, acts of arson, and kidnappings. In addition, the number of arson incidents, bombings, attacks on and assassinations of diplomats has increased in the past few years.

Although terrorists have made and often use more sophisticated explosive weapons, the majority of bombs are simple combustible devices. Rudimentary bombs in particular are easy to construct. Bombings typically need the least amount of group coordination, so they are one of the easiest terrorist tactics to employ. Additionally, they are relatively cheap; a terrorist group can get a considerable amount of attention by using bombs.

Terrorist Groups

As mentioned earlier, some terrorist organizations show considerable endurance, operating for a lengthy period, replacing their losses, preparing for new attacks, and turning into semipermanent subcultures. Other groups have fleeting existences. The MIPT/tkb database from July 2005 lists 792 terrorist organizations. Probably no more that 200, however, are active in any given year.

Over the past 37 years, most terrorist incidents are attributed to "Other Group" or "Unknown Group." This means that the organizational affiliation could not be positively identified. In situations where the organization was positively identified, Hamas (446), Basque Fatherland and Freedom (ETA; 387), and the National Liberation Army (in Columbia; 282) have committed the greatest number of incidents. Those groups responsible for the highest number of fatalities are al Qaeda (3,521), Hezbollah (821), Tanzim Qa'idat al-Jihad fi Bilad al-Rafidayn, a Palestinian group (615), and Hamas (577).

EXPLORING THE CAUSES

The field of terrorism research lacks rigorous studies that address its causes. Nevertheless, when causes are examined, most explanations fall into three categories: structural, psychological, and rational choice. Ultimately, terrorism is a synergistic phenomenon with causes that interact with effects, and these responses are then ultimately connected to causes.[137]

Total Terrorist Events by Tactic, January 1, 1968–July 30, 2005

TACTIC	INCIDENTS	INJURIES	FATALITIES
Armed Attack	3,657	10,318	5,604
Arson	868	297	367
Assassination	2,182	955	2,762
Barricade/Hostage	201	2,198	896
Bombing	13,217	60,274	15,293
Hijacking	232	377	475
Kidnapping	1,652	135	736
Other	152	385	231
Police	1	6	4
Unconventional Attack	56	103	3,004
Unknown	239	197	270
TOTAL	22,457	75,245	29,642

Figure 4.4 **Terrorists and terrorist groups employ a variety of tactics to commit their attacks. This chart shows how many times different tactics were used and the total number of attacks from 1968 to 2005.**

EXAMINING THE EFFECTS

Terrorism has numerous structural and psychological effects on victims, citizens, observers, practitioners, and politicians, ranging from death to numbness. None of the effects are mutually exclusive; a person or organization may experience a broad continuum of effects at various times during and after a terrorist incident. Moreover, some of the factors that explain the

Incidents Attributed to Major Terrorist Groups, January 1, 1968–July 30, 2005

GROUP	INCIDENTS	INJURIES	FATALITIES
Abu Nidal Organization (ANO)	82	654	210
Abu Sayaf Group (ASG)	52	491	197
al-Fatah	198	1,322	417
al-Qaeda	27	6,476	3,521
Amal	69	65	67
Anti-Castro Cubans	213	55	86
Armed Islamic Group	64	359	506
Armenian Army for the Liberation of Armenia (ASALA)	78	269	46
Basque Fatherland and Freedom (ETA)	387	538	61
Black September	92	132	30
Communist Party of Nepal-Maoists	261	292	133
DHKP-C (Devrimci Sol)	73	90	20
Earth Liberation Front	50	0	0
Front di Liberazione Naziunale di a Corsica (FLNC)	116	27	0
Hamas	446	2,787	577
Hezbollah	176	1,475	821
Irish Republican Army (IRA	83	139	28
Jewish Defense League (JDL)	72	37	5
Kurdistan Worker's Party	83	211	38
Liberation Tigers of Tamil Eelam (LTTE)	72	2,431	514
Manuel Rodriguez Patriotic Front	51	15	1
National Liberation Army (Columbia)	282	202	124
New People's Army (NPA)	78	48	67
Other Group	2,028	7,935	3,483
Palestine Liberation Organization	62	588	39
Palestinian Islamic Jihad (PIJ)	66	663	134
People's War Group (PWG) (India)	75	122	112
Popular Front for the Liberation of Palestine	103	646	163
Red Army Faction	41	62	3
Revolutionary Armed Forces of Columbia	455	1,000	450
Shining Path	136	265	130
Taliban	118	205	213
Tanzim Qa'idat al-Jihad fi Bilad al-Rafidayn	117	1,302	615
Tupac Amaru Revolutionary Movement	105	21	20
Unknown Group	13,068	25,172	10,648

Figure 4.5 **Not all acts of terrorism are claimed by, or can be traced to, known terrorism groups. This table shows how many attacks from 1968 to 2005 can be attributed to different groups.**

effects of terrorism are intimately connected to its decline.[138] When looking at why terrorism will end in any context, we should acknowledge the possibility of its related concept of terrorism declining.

DECLINE

In order to understand the decline of terrorism, we must have a sense of why a particular terrorist movement appeared and what effect it had. Conditions leading to the rise and the decline of terrorism are interdependent. In particular, variables responsible for its decline are conceptually related to those important in causing it.

Although the causes for the rise of terrorism have been discussed elsewhere,[139] it is wise to take into consideration the notion of decline. Essentially, decline is a complimentary effect of terrorism. The general order of importance for each variable, however, differs for each terrorist group.

Two arguments specifically address the causes of decline. On the one hand, Ross and Gurr give theoretical reasons for the decline of domestic political terrorism in advanced industrialized societies where this phenomenon has occurred, using Canada and the United States as examples.[140] They have determined that the following four general conditions contribute to the decline of political terrorism: preemption (catching and stopping the perpetrators before the act occurs), deterrence (convincing the terrorists not to act), burnout, and backlash. On the other hand, Crenshaw contends that "explanations of the decline of terrorism must be derived from statements about the causes."[141] She surveyed 40 organizations that commit terrorism and developed the following three categories of reasons for decline: defeat, strategic shift, and disintegration for internal purposes. She argues that "[t]hree categories of factors [are] important to these patterns: the background conditions that structure the conflict between government and challenger, the characteristics of the organization practicing terrorism, and the policy response of the government."[142]

In general, both arguments fail to comprehensively examine the causes of terrorism, the literature on prevention, and the reasons why other types of political conflicts end. The previous arguments can be extended and qualified in a number of respects. New variables should be examined and integrated with the ones already mentioned by Ross and Gurr, and Crenshaw, so that a better model or theory ran be developed, and hypotheses derived from these efforts can be tested.

To accomplish this task, we need to see the decline of political terrorism as a multistage process, to which eight factors contribute. Much like the causes of terrorism in general, these variables can be divided between the preconditions and things that precipitate the terrorism. Deterrence, accommodation, and counterterrorist tactics can be considered the preconditions. Death of terrorists, imprisonment, individual burnout, group disintegration, and support impairment are the precipitants for decline. These practices can operate independently and interdependently.[143] Three interdependent or complimentary reasons explain why terrorism changes: morphing, lifecycles, and stages.

MORPHING

The different types of terrorism are not totally exclusive or static. Often, there is a pattern whereby state terrorism provokes individuals to engage in domestic terrorism, which in turn leads to international terrorism. This pattern, referred to as morphing, describes the existence of groups and countries where terrorism has persisted. For example, shortly after the establishment of the state of Israel (1948), its army's violent actions against the Palestinian population led to Palestinian terrorism, which contributed to the internationalization of Palestinian political violence to gain publicity for their struggle.[144] Similarly, in many Central American countries (such as

Nicaragua and El Salvador), government oppression against workers and peasants led to the formation of guerrilla organizations during the 1980s. These organizations, in turn, used terrorist tactics against the military.[145]

Terrorist groups often shift from committing domestic operations to orchestrating international incidents because the latter attract more attention, publicity, and recognition, and larger audiences. Moving its activities abroad may help a terrorist organization avoid detection or capture, create additional fear beyond its traditional base of operations, garner more resources, obtain easier access to vulnerable targets, and ultimately help achieve its objectives more quickly. A group may also commit terrorist acts in another state because the possibility of getting caught is minimized.

With regard to morphing, it is also important to understand that many terrorist groups have a lifecycle. This has implications for their actions, changes in membership, goals, and activities. Terrorist organizations mature or age and, over time, become more sophisticated. This process can be thought of as a life cycle. Through this process, and unless their ranks have not been decimated by arrests, deaths, or disaffection, terrorist groups typically get better at what they do, particularly because they learn from their successes and failures. In sum, new members join the organization, commit violent actions, get arrested, burn out, settle down, and mature out of terrorism.

Morphing and the cyclical nature of terrorism can occur not only at the group level, but also on a geographic level, incorporating both countries and regions alike. Naturally, these two concepts frustrate attempts to understand and combat terrorism.

Rapoport

According to Rapoport, over the past 120 years there have been four waves of terrorism. Each had different causes, tactics and reasons for decline:

In the 1880s an initial 'anarchist wave' appeared that continued for some 40 years. Its successor, the "anticolonial wave," began in the 1920s and by the 1960s had largely disappeared. The late 1960s witnessed the birth of the 'new left wave' which dissipated largely in the 1990s leaving a few groups still active in Sri Lanka, Spain, France, Peru, and Columbia. The fourth, or 'religious wave,' began in 1979 and if it follows the patterns of its predecessors it still has twenty-five years to run.[146]

He equates this phenomenon with a

human life cycle pattern, where dreams that inspire fathers lose their attractiveness for the sons. Clearly, the life cycle of the waves does not correspond to those of organizations. Organizations normally dissipate before the wave does, though sometimes an organization survives its associated wave. . . . By way of comparison, the average life of organizations in the third or new left wave is two years.[147]

On the surface, Rapoport's explanation makes sense; however, not every time frame conforms to the description or criteria. For example, both the Irish and Palestinian struggles that have resorted to terrorism have their origins in the 1800s. Thus, they have lasted considerably longer than 25 years.

Hewitt

Hewitt, in an attempt to test whether terrorism is fostered because politicians ignore requests or because they pander to them, identifies the following four waves of terrorism in the United States: Southern White Supremacist (1955–1972); Black Militants (1965–1974); revolutionary/left-wing terrorism (1969–1977), and (1977–1995).[148] He says,

Based on the American experience, . . . sustained out-
breaks of terrorism are associated with the existence of
a substantial body of sympathizers and supporters. In
all the four cases examined, a sizable number of people
felt very strongly about some social/political issue-
segregation, racial equality, the Vietnam war, abortion-
and also felt that the political system ignored, or was
hostile to, their concerns. [149]

Weinberg and Pedahzur

Finally, Weinberg and Pedahzur have outlined the conditions
under which terrorist groups suspend violent activities and join
or form political parties. In short, they suggest that "a transfor-
mation in the prevailing political order," "state repression," "the
problems of clandestinely," and "government amnesty" are major
factors that encourage this practice.[150]

CONCLUSION

By reviewing the history and the reasons why terrorist groups
form and continue to commit acts of political violence, we can
determine similarities and differences in the patterns of their
causes. Consequently, this analysis points to the powerful effects
of grievances. Although the factors discussed here are important, none can sustain an organization without the perception
of some sort of widely felt and long-standing hurt or damage
to a group, culture, race, or ethnic group. Unresolved grievances
have been a source of contention despite changes in leaders and
generations.[151] Unless some sort of meaningful accommodation
is made, conflicts will persist and possibly get worse, bringing
with it new generations to carry on the struggle through sense-
less property destruction, injury, and death to innocent people.

CHAPTER 5

WHAT DOES THE FUTURE HOLD?

INTRODUCTION

One of everyone's biggest fears is that, following the 9/11 incidents, heightened security measures will be relaxed and people will become less vigilant. The concrete barriers will slowly and inconspicuously be removed from prominent federal government buildings and transportation hubs. The increased precautions for access control that we have instituted at airports and entrances will also be lifted. This, of course, would be the perfect time for another terrorist attack.

The events of 9/11 have demonstrated that America, the world's largest superpower, is not invincible. Many people thought the United States would never be attacked on its home soil by foreign-based terrorists. If 19 individuals can cause so much damage and wreak so much havoc armed only with their fists—and, in some cases, box cutters—we need to rethink our country's approach to counterterrorism. Americans can no longer assume they are immune from terrorist attacks at home. In order to deal with this insecurity, we will have to spend valuable resources and challenge values we hold dear, including our cherished and protected civil liberties, which we will have to partially forfeit in order to maintain some degree of heightened security.

Recent attacks may foreshadow some of the possible terrorism that many countries could be subjected to in the coming years. We have found that a variety of structures and systems are susceptible to terrorist attacks, and innocent civilians can be hurt or lose their lives in many different ways. The possibility of biological, chemical, and nuclear attacks (especially because the 9/11 terrorists were checking out crop dusters as "delivery vehicles") increase already high levels of fear and paranoia. In short, America is a changed nation, and its citizens and national security network may never be the same. For those who believe that terrorism will continue, then we must redouble our efforts. A variety of strategies, used in combination, have been mobilized to prevent, deter, respond to, and combat terrorism.

Unfortunately, on the other hand, many Americans fail to realize that the federal government, at the behest of the current administration, may be using the 9/11 disaster to strengthen and expand what can be called the "national security state." Several of the national security proposals in place today, which were hastily considered and passed, "have been on the table," hidden in file cabinets for a considerable period of time, only to be dusted off and put into effect now. To preserve our Western democracy and freedoms, we need to avoid panicky or knee-jerk responses that are intended more for symbolic than practical reasons, especially if we are to avoid adverse "unintended consequences."

Mourners visit Ground Zero during a ceremony marking the one-year anniversary of the September 11 attacks on the World Trade Center. The aftermath of the attacks has left Americans much more conscious of the threat of terrorism domestically and abroad.

In sum, we need countermeasures to fight terrorism and actively seek out terrorists. We need to do so, however, in an intelligent and rational manner; we need to act slowly and wisely. In short, can we ever go back to the way we used to be? The answer is no. Are we any safer now than we were on September 11, 2001? Maybe. We have done much to protect ourselves, but more remains to be done—and there is still much more that we should not do. Should we refuse to be reactive and avoid playing into the strategy of the terrorists by retaining our freedoms, our democratic values? Unquestionably, yes.

In the study of terrorism, when commenting on the future, there are two basic perspectives: optimistic and pessimistic. In an optimistic scenario, the frequency, intensity, and lethality of terrorism will subside to a point where it is perceived to be a thing of the past. In the pessimistic alternative, terrorism will increase, and those committing it will eventually resort to utilizing more dangerous and destructive weapons of mass destruction. In between these two extremes are multiple positions.

In general, despite a worldwide effort to clamp down on terrorist groups and their activities, the frequency of terrorist acts will probably be greater then it has been in the past for three important reasons. Uncompromising leaders and governments will frustrate less powerful citizens and groups, who may then resort to terrorism. Administrations not wishing all-out warfare may sponsor terrorism. In addition, weapons and communications technology will be more readily accessible to terrorists.

Simultaneously, as many conflict theorists have argued, full-scale war is becoming obsolete; it is being replaced by skirmishes, border clashes, and terrorism. Increasingly, militaries are becoming more sophisticated, destructive, and accurate in their targeting, thus leading to increased military power. Governments, however, may be reluctant to use comprehensive military action because they fear retaliation. This may motivate leaders to realize that it is not necessary to resort to military action. A simple threat by some countries will defeat aggressors.

Finally, advances in destructive and communicative technologies have made them smaller and cheaper, and thus more available to terrorist organizations. Those individuals and groups who could not afford to mount a terrorist campaign might now have access to more sophisticated and deadlier weapons. Improvements in communications may help terrorist groups link to one another. This will lead to more extravagant, attention-seeking, vicious acts and to the possibility that terrorists will use more destructive technologies, such as nuclear, biological, chemical, and toxic weapons.

FUTURE TYPES OF TERRORISM: THE THREAT OF BIOLOGICAL, CHEMICAL AND NUCLEAR TERRORISM

The United States is especially concerned about terrorists constructing, obtaining, and using WMDs—and for good reason.

Beginning in the late 1960s, security and terrorist analysts warned about the possibility of chemical, biological, and nuclear attacks by terrorists and their organizations.[152] Analysts also cautioned against mass hysteria, because terrorist organizations lacked the ability to deliver these WMDs without getting injured or killing themselves, or incurring the same fate to a great number of people in the development and construction of the weapons.

Although WMDs are supposed to be confined to warfare among states, and a number of conventions controlling its use are in place (such as the Nuclear Non-Proliferation Treaty [NPT]), the use of WMDs by terrorists (also known as asymmetric terrorism), remains a source of concern for arms-control experts, public safety officials, and the public at large.[153] It is also understood that, with the advent of suicide terrorism, fear of being killed while delivering a WMD is probably less of a worry for some terrorists and their organizations. A number of incidents, not only in the United States, but elsewhere, speak to the capability of terrorist groups using these techniques in relatively controlled settings.

In the United States, in 1972, members of the Order of the Rising Sun, an American fascist group, were caught with 80 pounds of typhoid bacteria cultures, which they planned to add to several cities' water supplies.[154] In September 1984, individuals from the Rajneeshee cult, who owned a large tract of land in Oregon, poisoned local salad bars with *Salmonella typhimurium*. They wanted to make the locals sick, so they would not take part in a critical vote.[155] Again, in 1985, police arrested a group of American neo-Nazis, who were in possession of 30 gallons of cyanide they were planning to use to poison the water in New York City and Washington, D.C.[156] In 1995, three incidents were uncovered where white supremist groups in the United States, or individuals with links to these organizations, possessed deadly biological agents.[157] And in 1998, Larry Wayne Harris, once a member of a neo-Nazi organization, legally obtained anthrax and was accused of attempting to attack the New York City subway system with it.

Outside the United States, several incidents in which individuals and groups possessed materials or made threats of using WMDs have caused counterterrorist planners to take pause. During the 1980s, the Animal Liberation Front (ALF) claimed to have placed rat poison in Mars candy bars. Similar scares, including injecting toxic mercury into turkeys sold to supermarkets during Thanksgiving and Christmas, have occurred and have been attributed to the ALF.[158] Another incident is the previously mentioned 1995 sarin gas attack in the Tokyo subway by members of the Aum Shinrikyo religious cult. This incident left 12 people dead and 12,000 injured. Also in 1995, Shamil Basayev, the leader of a Chechen rebel group, buried a container of radioactive cesium in a popular park in Moscow.

Regardless, very few terrorist organizations have resorted to the use of WMDs. Two important obstacles stand in the way: lack of technical sophistication, and motivational and organizational drawbacks of individuals and counterterrorist organizations. According to Stern, "The technical hurdles would be considerable: acquiring the agent or weapon would present one set of difficulties; disseminating or exploding it would present another."[159] Others are less sanguine. According to Laqueur,

> There is much reason to believe that if such attacks should be carried out in the near future, many, perhaps the great majority, will fail, or will have a smaller effect than anticipated. But it should also be clear that if only one out of ten, one out of a hundred such attempts succeeds, the damage caused, the number of victims will be infinitely higher than at anytime in the past.[160]

The more immediate threat, however, is terrorism in connection with the U.S. presence in Iraq.

FUTURE MOTIVATORS

Large bureaucracies, like most governments and corporations, will fail to address the continual unmet needs of domestic and/or indigenous groups and workers.[161] Both the increasing tendency toward big bureaucracy and the practice of making processes routine[162] take away the ability of groups opposed to policies and practices to receive formal or informal access to and by government agencies. This lack of access may then frustrate their ability to work within the system and may motivate these groups to use violence in an attempt to have their grievances addressed.

Around the world, small civil wars, population growth, natural disasters, conflicting values, and nonexistent or unequal access to food, employment, and natural resources (through destruction and depletion) are prime motivators for mass migrations, refugee problems, and unaddressed grievances. Over time, these factors will place a greater burden on governments.

Some of these issues are attributable to the seemingly perpetual north-south and socio-economic gaps. All these factors, in combination, may fuel the future course of terrorism. Which individuals or groups, though, might in the future continue or begin to resort to terrorism?

FUTURE PERPETRATORS

The spread of Islamic fundamentalism will not end and may, in fact, increase. Secular governments, such as those in Algeria and the Philippines, or ones that are ruled by monarchs (in Jordan and Saudi Arabia) are being challenged by indigenous religious fundamentalists that resort to violence to back up their demands. It does not appear that the Palestinian/Israeli conflict will end anytime soon. Perhaps when Hamas and the Al-Aqsa Martyrs' Brigade cease terrorist activities and new leaders emerge, there may be an opportunity for true peace. Until that time, however, the conflict will likely persist.

Fringe members of the antiglobalist movement may, for a variety of reasons, strike out with terrorism. The violent outbursts in Seattle (1999), Québec City (2001), Gothenburg (2001), and Genoa (2001), where members of the International Monetary Fund were meeting, has led analysts to believe that some of the antiglobalist terrorist groups will escalate the intensity of their attacks in the years to come.

Over the past decade, the number of nationalist and ethnic groups that are seeking independence from their home countries has increased. Tensions among certain nationalities, especially among Indians, Sikhs, and Pakistanis, are bubbling below the surface. The Pakistani army, in their efforts to root out suspected Taliban and al Qaeda members among the isolated tribes along the Pakistan-Afghanistan border, is fostering anti-Pakistani sentiments. Finally, there has been talk of something called the "Third Position," "a coalition between the extreme left and extreme right, between nationalism and socialism."[163] In other words, the number of perpetrators and the causes that could motivate—and even unite them—is limitless.

Finally, we will have to deal with single-issue terrorism. History has demonstrated that occasionally, appropriately motivated individuals are willing to resort to terrorism in the United States and elsewhere. This has been particularly evident in the last two decades, during which time members of the Animal Liberation Front, pro-life movement, the Jewish Defense League, and ecoterrorists have all committed acts of terrorism.

THE WAR IN IRAQ

The United States' and Great Britain's military (and political) efforts in Iraq could have one of three possible effects. They might help pave the way toward stabilizing the country and perhaps the Middle East-Persian Gulf region, leading to a decrease in terrorism. If Western-style democracy manages to take hold, perhaps Iraq could be an example for the neighboring countries of Iran and Syria. On the other hand, it has been reported that Islamic Fundamantalist terrorists are flocking to Iraq to prove once again that the United States is not invincible.

The American and British occupation of Iraq may serve as a warning to countries that have sponsored terrorism, or acted as a safe haven for terrorists, to stop these kinds of activities. This is what many commentators ascribe to Libya's 2004 desire to give up its nuclear weapons testing program, its admission of responsibility for the Lockerbie attack (December 1988), and its normalization of relations with the United States.

Then again, the presence of foreign troops in Iraq is increasing hostility and resentment toward the United States and Great Britain from moderate Iraqis and citizens of other Middle Eastern countries. They think that Americans and Brits should not be there in the first place and, further disapprove because now that Americans and Brits are there, they are having considerable difficulty restoring order. Since the invasion, a phenomenal number of innocent civilians have been injured or killed.[164] Most people are still unemployed, and adequate food, utilities, and medical care are lacking. Prisoners in the Abu Ghraib prison are being held and questioned, and some have been tortured (in violation of the Geneva Convention).[165] The U.S. and British presence in Iraq—particularly without the support of the United Nations, and the fact that, to date, no WMDs have been found there, as claimed—is being perceived as yet another example of America using its power (and military might) in an arbitrary and inappropriate fashion. This perception increases with each day that the United States and Great Britain stay in Iraq.

SOLUTIONS

The future is unpredictable. A number of changes should take place to minimize the possibility of terrorism and lessen the amount of property damage, injuries, and deaths when attacks do occur. Most doctors diagnosing a sick patient suggest that a coherent and clear communication of the problem is half the battle toward a cure. This phenomenon has often been lacking in studies on terrorism. Thus, more rigorous, nonideological, sophisticated, and theoretically appropriate research into under-standing terrorism is needed to prevent pointless destruction of lives and property.

What Is Not Going to Help

Although bilateral treaties and cooperation among countries in the fight against terrorism occur, the problem of sharing intelligence, not only inside a country but also beyond, is a real one. It is doubtful that this problem will be solved in the near future.

We have also learned, particularly in the cases of Libya and Cuba, that diplomatic and economic sanctions are not sufficient to deter countries from helping terrorist groups.

Poorly thought-out or designed technological fixes, such as facial recognition systems that are derived from biometric screening, will probably not help in deterring or detecting possible terrorists. Post-9/11 anti-terrorism technology, as it currently exists, is subject to considerable error. Although these methods may be appropriate for a controlled setting, they are not easily applied to the real world. Law enforcement currently utilizes multiple screening systems, including driver's licenses, passports, fingerprints, and DNA. In other words, we already have many viable options for catching suspects.

Another idea, proposed in the immediate wake of 9/11, was for national ID cards to be issued. This suggestion was hotly debated; its civil liberties infringements were highlighted before it was ultimately rejected.

Finally, target hardening will not deter the most dedicated individuals from attacking. Until more sophisticated antiter-rorist measures are taken, though, it is the least risky first step in an antiterrorism strategy. It seems, however, that there is often little the authorities can do to prevent terrorist attacks, especially those carried out by terrorists with religious moti-vations.[166] This is especially true when advocacy for terrorism emanates some 6,000 miles away, in a theocracy.

What May Help

What is going to win the day in the fight against terrorism? Clearly, a multipronged approach is most appropriate. One way of minimizing future attacks is to address the legitimate grievances of the terrorists.[167] For example, in April 2003, the United States finally announced that it would remove the nearly 5,000 troops that have been stationed in Saudi Arabia since the 1991 Gulf War. This was one of the longstanding demands of the al Qaeda network.[168]

Another suggestion has been the collection and timely analysis of better intelligence, both human and technologically gathered so that attacks can be prevented and perpetrators can be caught. Technology can only do so much, however. Thus, in terms of intelligence, countries will need to rely more on good informants. The secretive nature of antiterrorist organizations, including the inability to cultivate appropriate sources, and the lack of expertise in appropriate foreign languages, makes it difficult for many intelligence agencies to obtain detailed information on terrorist groups. This information, when collected, however, needs to be gathered in a manner that protects people's civil liberties, while not providing those who aim to harm us with an unfair advantage. States are also well advised to develop a national database to track suspected terrorists and to allow criminal justice agencies to integrate the appropriate infrastructure for it to be useful.

Often neglected are the personal motivations of law enforcement officers in identifying possible terrorist suspects. In other words, those officers who are truly attentive and who genuinely care about their job be will more likely to catch terrorist suspects.

Some have suggested that now is the time for Americans to take a serious look at how they are viewed throughout the world. Perhaps the United States should examine its foreign policies and practices and revise them so the country does not continuously aggravate foreign states. America must respect the sovereign rights of other countries and cannot continue to support authoritarian, totalitarian, or fascist regimes when it is temporarily convenient. At the same time, the United States must not force democracy on those states who do not wish to have it, or perhaps are not ready to embrace its benefits. Unilateral decisions (or pacts made with a handful of countries), similar to what transpired in Iraq, only reinforce

Muslim Dislike of Americans in Saudi Arabia

During the 1980s, throughout the Middle East and in countries where there are large Muslim populations (e.g., Afghanistan, Indonesia, and Malaysia), there was a revival of Muslim fundamentalism. Fundamentalism basically stresses the importance of Islamic practices with regard to the role of women in society, politics, and the laws that govern countries inhabited by Muslims. In 1990, in response to Iraq's invasion of Kuwait, the United States stationed troops in Saudi Arabia. At one time, there were approximately 500,000 American soldiers living there. The Saudis, despite internal grumblings, were only too happy to assist, as they feared that Saddam Hussein's regime would target their country next. Many Muslims consider Saudi Arabia to be the birthplace of their religion, and, according to Muslim lore, members of the House of Saud (the Saudi ruling family) are considered to be the protectors of these holy places.

At the end of the Gulf War in 1991, the United States failed to remove its troops from Saudi Arabia. Mecca and Medina, the holy cities of Islam, are located in Saudi Arabia. Some argue that America's presence near the holy sites, almost a decade after the end of the war, was so galling to Muslim fundamentalists, that it was one of the alleged causes of the 9/11 attacks.

In April 2003, after 13 years on Saudi soil, the United States announced that it was removing its troops. Unfortunately, this action has not stopped fundamentalists from engaging in terrorist attacks against Saudi and American targets.

the perception of poor decision making in the United States. Major foreign-policy decisions, like the war in Iraq, should have been made with the increased cooperation of the member states of the United Nations and with the cooperation of other important nongovernmental organizations. America needs to admit to the world that it has been on the wrong side of many of the world's conflicts. Since the Cold War, regardless of the continent, the United States has supported many authoritarian or fascist regimes.[169]

These sentiments extend to American and transnational corporations. Although most advanced industrialized democracies provide aid to many lesser-developed countries, business interests are often quick to exploit these settings.[170] American corporations are continuously perceived to be exploitive and insensitive. For example, it is no secret that people in lesser-developed countries, working in sweatshop-like conditions, make brand-name products (for companies such as Gap, Banana Republic, and Nike) for purchase by consumers in advanced industrialized countries.[171] These economic decisions have long-term unintended consequences that many corporate directors, shareholders, and consumers are willing to overlook in the interest of expediency and temporary financial gain.

Most Americans are proud of their culture and the nation's progress, and rightly so. This stance, however, leads many Americans to display an attitude of superiority. When traveling abroad, Americans need to learn more about the countries and cultures they visit, rather than being as close-minded as they often are. The problem of the "ugly American" has not been lost on many observers of anti-Americanism. Americans need to be more humble and accommodating.

Unless other countries contribute (either financially or materially) to the war on terrorism, the United States will continue to feel marginalized. In an effort to deal with the increased expenditures for terrorism, perhaps the U.S. government should institute a terrorism tax. This way, the public would have a better understanding of where its money is going. This might also force politicians to do something about our aggressive international posture

TOLERATING TERRORISM

Perhaps there is not much we can do when individuals and groups are so firmly committed to the idea and practice of overthrowing the values, institutions, and government of the United States. Maybe all we can do is bury our heads in the sand, or engage in mindless hedonism, because we believe that "the end is near." During the 1970s, the survivalist movement, for example, was a response to the fear many Americans had of widespread civil and racial unrest in our cities. Some commentators have suggested that the 9/11 attacks narrowed the racial divide in the United States. In other words, traditional antipathy between blacks and whites may have temporarily subsided because of a shared or common enemy.

Regardless of which measure(s) we take, there will be costs (financial, psychological, and political) attached to each of these proposals. One of the most debated measures is the idea of developing a country where the surveillance of citizens (particularly through the use of closed-circuit television) appears pervasive. Americans, used to broad protections of privacy, will have considerable difficulty with this new state of affairs. Having their privacy curtailed or giving it up will not come easily.

Finally, although terrorism has created a considerable amount of controversy and has cost governments and corporations substantial resources, perhaps there is a tolerable level of terrorism with which a society can live.[172] For example, during the 1960s and 1970s, citizens in advanced industrialized countries were constantly reminded, through the media, educators, and personal experience, that street crime was increasing. This created a furor of public indignation and governmental responses, which manifested as a "war on crime."

Although the rate of crime has increased since these times, the crisis seems, over time, to have abated, or to have been replaced by the "war on terrorism." Similarly, and building on the work of Durkheim, no one has seriously posed the question of whether or not there are tolerable levels of violence under which we can still live.

Terrorist attacks are disruptive to the normal functioning of government, business, and people's daily lives. Policymakers and practitioners, as much as possible, need to avoid simplistic responses, however. Why? Because many of these answers lead to the needless expenditure of resources, and some are actually quite dangerous.

I hope that this book has provided a similar process and the suggestions outlined here will allow us to minimize the occurrence of terrorism and prevent researchers, policymakers, and practitioners from going down blind alleys or targeting as terrorists those individuals and groups who engage in legitimate advocacy, protest, and dissent. Needless to say, we must recognize that, in some places, there is absolutely nothing the United States, or any other country, can do. In these cases, neither accommodation nor eradication of terrorist enclaves will stem the tide of terrorism.

Terrorism has not disappeared. Increasing separatism and ethnic conflict in the former Communist states and satellites of the Soviet Union and elsewhere, and the tendency of some religious fundamentalists (Muslim, Christian, Catholic, Protestant, and Sikh, for example) to use acts of terrorism, will provide an up-to-date laboratory with which to study and combat terrorism well into the twenty-first century.

Chapter 1
Introduction

1 Although no internationally accepted definition of terrorism exists, this author uses Schmid's (1983) consensus definition of terrorism. Alex P. Schmid, *Political Terrorism: A Research Guide to Concepts, Theories, Data Bases and Literature.* New Brunswick, NJ: Transaction Books, 1983.

   With a few clarifications, the original definition meets the purposes of most researchers, policymakers, and practitioners. See, for example, Jeffrey Ian Ross, "An Events Data Base on Political Terrorism in Canada: Some Conceptual and Methodological Problems," *Conflict Quarterly* 8(1988)2: pp. 47–64; Jeffrey Ian Ross, "Attributes of Domestic Political Terrorism in Canada, 1960-1985," *Terrorism: An International Journal* 11(1988)3: pp. 214–233; Jeffrey Ian Ross, "The Nature of Contemporary International Terrorism," in David Charters, ed. *Democratic Responses to International Terrorism.* Ardsely, NY: Transnational Publishers, 1991, pp. 17–42.

2 Jeffrey Ian Ross, *The Dynamics of Political Crime.* Thousand Oaks, CA: Sage Publications, 2002, Chapter 5; Jessica Stern, *The Ultimate Terrorists.* Cambridge, MA: Harvard University Press, 1999, pp. 8–10.

3 Mary L. Dudziak, ed. *September 11 in History: A Watershed Moment?* Durham, NC: Duke University Press, 2003.

4 Michael Griffin, *Reaping the Whirlwind: Afghanistan, Al Qa'ida and the Holy War.* London: Pluto Press, 2003; Rohan Gunaratna, *Inside Al Qaeda: Global Network of Terror.* New York: Columbia University Press, 2002; Jason Burke, *Al Qaeda: Casting a Shadow of Terror.* London: I. B. Tauris, 2003.

5 Simon Reeve, *The New Jackals.* Boston: Northeastern University Press, 1999, p. 15.

6 For further analysis of this interpretation, see, for example, Michael Moore's movie *Fahrenheit 9/11.*

7 U.S. Printing Office, *The 9/11 Commission Report.* New York: W.W. Norton, 2004.

8 Jeffrey Ian Ross, "Post 9/11: Are We Any Safer Now?" in Lynne L. Snowden and Bradley C. Whitsel, eds. *Terrorism: Research, Readings, and Realities.* Upper Saddle River, NJ: Prentice Hall, 2005, pp. 380–389; Jeffrey Ian Ross, "Reacting to 9/11: Rational Policy and Practice Versus Threat of the Week Syndrome," in Graham Walker and David Charters, eds., *After 9/11: Terrorism and Crime in a Globalized World.* Joint Publication of the UNB's Centre for Conflict Studies and Dalhousie University's Center for Foreign Policy Studies, 2005, pp. 306–321.

9 Jeffrey Ian Ross and Reuben J. Miller, "The Effects of Oppositional Political Terrorism: Five Actor-based Models," *Low Intensity Conflict and Law Enforcement* 6(1997)3: pp. 76–107.

10 Mary Buckley and Rick Fawn, eds., *Global Responses to Terrorism: 9/11 Afghanistan and Beyond.* New York: Routledge, 2003.

11 It also did not help to have a handful of yet-unsolved anthrax threats, nor a youth who went throughout the American West leaving pipe bombs in rural mailboxes.

12 See, for example, Grant Wardlaw, *Political Terrorism: Theory, Tactics, and Counter Measures.* New York: Cambridge University Press, 1982; Christopher Hewitt, *The Effectiveness of Anti-terrorist Policies.* Lanham, MD: University Press of America, 1984; Leonard Weinberg and Paul B. Davis,

Introduction to Political Terrorism. New York: McGraw Hill, 1989, Chapters 5–7; Sederberg, Peter C. Sederberg, *Terrorist Myths Illusion, Rhetoric, and Reality,* Englewood Cliffs, NJ: Prentice Hall, 1989, Chapter 6.

13 See, for example, Neil C. Livingstone and Terrell E. Arnold, eds., *Fighting Back: Winning the War Against Terrorism.* Toronto: Lexington Books, 1986.

14 For example, Manus I. Midlarsky, Martha Crenshaw, and Fumihiko Yoshida, "Why Violence Spreads: The Contagion of International Terrorism," *International Studies Quarterly* 24(1980): pp. 262–298.

15 To the best of my knowledge, no similar studies were done of Washington (actually Arlington, VA, where the Pentagon is located) and rural Pennsylvania—the other sites of the attacks.

16 Andrew Arno, "Communication, Conflict, and Storylines: The News Media as Actors in a Cultural Context," in Andrew Arno and Wimal Dissanayake, eds., *The News Media in National and International Conflict.* Boulder, CO: Westview Press, 1984, pp. 1.

17 Arno, "Communication, Conflict, and Storylines," p. 3.

18 Brian Jenkins, *International Terrorism: A New Mode of Conflict.* Santa Monica: RAND Corporation, 1974.

19 Bruce Hoffman, 1998. *Inside Terrorism,* Chapter 5. New York: Columbia University Press, 1998.

20 Philip Jenkins, *Moral Panic.* New Haven, CT: Yale University Press, 1998.

21 Alex Schmid and Janny de Graaf, *Violence as Communication: Insurgent Terrorism and the Western News Media.* Beverly Hills, CA: Sage Publications, 1982.

22 Mark Fishman, *Manufacturing the News.* Austin: University of Texas Press, 1980.

23 Joel Best, ed., *Images of Issues: Typifying Contemporary Social Problems.* New York: Aldine De Gruyter, 1989; Joel Best, *Random Violence: How We Talk About New Crimes and New Victims.* Los Angeles, CA: University of California Press, 1999.

24 Jenkins, *Moral Panic;* Philip Jenkins, *Images of Terror: What We Can and Can't Know About Terrorism.* Hawthorne, NY: Aldine de Gruyer, 2003.

25 Weinberg and Davis, *Introduction to Political Terrorism,* Chapter 2.

26 Max Taylor, *The Terrorist.* London: Brassey's Defense Publishers, 1988, p. 38.

27 Walter Laqueur, *Terrorism.* Boston: Little, Brown, 1977, p. 17.

28 Ibid.

29 These countries include the United States, Canada, the United Kingdom, France, Germany, the Netherlands, Belgium, Spain, Italy, Israel, and Japan.

30 Louis Fournier, *FLQ: The Anatomy of an Underground Movement.* Toronto: NC Press, 1984.

31 Walter Laqueur, *No End to War: Terrorism in the Twenty-first Century.* New York: Continuum, 2003, p. 101.

32 Laqueur, *No End to War,* p. 101.

33 It is important to understand that, although the United Kingdom shares the same laws and currency, it consists of four territories: England, Wales, Scotland, and Northern Ireland.

Chapter 2
Terrorism Will End: Groups That Disbanded or Were Decimated

34 Leonard Weinberg and Ami Pedahzur, *Political Parties and Terrorist Groups.* New York: Routledge, 2003, p. 67.

35 Hoffman, *Inside Terrorism,* pp. 50–51.

36 Ibid., p. 51.

37 Ibid., p. 54.

38 Ibid., p. 55.

39 Weinberg and Pedahzur, *Political Parties and Terrorist Groups,* p. 68.

40 Martha Crenshaw Hutchinson, *Revolutionary Terrorism: The FLN in Algeria, 1954–1962.* Stanford, CA: Hoover Institution, 1978.

41 Chris Marshall, "Terrorism in Cyprus," in Frank Shanty and Raymond Picquet, eds., *Encyclopedia of World Terrorism.* Armonk, NY: M.E. Sharpe, 1997, pp. 160–162.

42 Fournier, *FLQ*; Ross, 1995.

43 Laqueur, *Terrorism,* p. 13.

44 Michael Gunther, *Pursuing a Just Cause for Their People.* Westport, CT: Greenwood Publishing, 1986.

45 William Sater, "Violence and the Puerto Rican Separatist Movement," *Terrorism, Violence, and Insurgency Report* 51(1984): pp. 4–10.

46 Committee on Government Reform, http://www.house.gov/reform/oversight/faln.htm.

47 See, for example, Ward Churchill and Jim Vander Wall, *Agents of Repression: The FBI's Secret War Against the Black Panther Party and the American Indian Movement.* Boston: South End, 1988.

48 Robert Tanenbaum and Philip Rosenberg, *Badge of the Assassin.* New York: New American Library, 1994.

49 Weinberg and Pedahzur, *Political Parties and Terrorist Groups,* p. 26.

50 Leonard Weinberg and William L. Eubank, *The Rise and Fall of Italian Terrorism.* Boulder, CO: Westview Press, 1987.

51 William R. Farrell, *Blood and Rage: The Story of the Japanese Red Army.* Lexington, MA: Lexington Books, 1990.

52 Jillian Becker, *Hitler's Children: The Story of the Baader-Meinhof Gang.* New York: Panther/Granada Books, 1978.

53 Michael Y. Dartnell, *Action Directe: Ultra-left Terrorism in France, 1979-1987.* London: Frank Cass, 2001.

54 Weinberg and Pedahzur, *Political Parties and Terrorist Groups,* pp. 84–85.

55 Vetter and Perlstein, *Perspectives on Terrorism,* p. 57.

56 Weinberg and Eubank, *The Rise and Fall of Italian Terrorism,* p. 3.

57 Ibid., pp. 35–37.

58 Ibid.

59 Vetter and Perlstein, *Perspectives on Terrorism,* p. 62.

60 Ibid.

61 Harold J. Vetter and Gary R. Perlstein, *Perspectives on Terrorism.* Pacific Grove, CA: Brooks/Cole Publishing, 1991, pp. 52–53.

62 Vetter and Perlstein, *Perspectives on Terrorism,* pp. 52–53.

63 Brent Smith, *Terrorism in America: Pipe Bombs and Pipe Dreams.* Albany: State University of New York Press, 1994, pp. 99–107.

64 This seems to be a regular feature of the current Palestinian–Israeli conflict.

65 Charles Townsend, *Terrorism: A Very Short Introduction.* New York: Oxford University Press, 2002, pp. 114–115.

66 See, for example, B. Hugh Tovar, "Active Response," in Uri Ra'anan, Robert L. Pfaltzgraff Jr., Richard H. Schultz, Ernst Halperin, and Igor Lukes, eds. *Hydra of Carnage.* Lexington, MA: Lexington Press, 1986, pp.

67 Townsend, *Terrorism,* pp. 120–121.

68 Ibid, p. 121.

69 Bruce Schneier, *Beyond Fear: Thinking Sensibly About Security in an Uncertain World.* New York: Copernicus Books, 2003.

Chapter 3
Terrorism Will Continue:
Groups That Still Exist

70 Martha Crenshaw, "How Terrorism Declines," *Terrorism and Political Violence* 3(1991)1: pp. 69–87.

71 James Aho, *The Politics of Righteousness: Idaho Christian Patriotism.* Seattle: University of Washington Press, 1990; Smith, *Terrorism in America,* Chapter 4.

72 In 1989, Pierce wrote *Hunter,* a follow-up book that espouses a blueprint for racists attacking African Americans.

73 For an insight into this incident, the reader might want to see the movie *Talk Radio.* Produced by controversial filmmaker Oliver Stone and featuring a performance by Eric Bogosian, the movie is loosely based on the now deceased KOA Denver radio talk show performances of Allen Berg. During the early 1980s, Berg used to demean, belittle, and incite his audience, among whom were white supremacists and neo-Nazis. He was gunned down in front of his home.

74 Vetter and Perlstein, *Perspectives on Terrorism,* p. 59.

75 Ibid., p. 60.

76 Smith, *Terrorism in America,* Chapter 4.

77 Mark. S. Hamm, *Apocalypse at Waco: Ruby Ridge and Waco Revenged.* Boston: Northeastern University Press, 1997.

78 There was an outstanding warrant for the arrest of Weaver, an anti-Semite who attended Aryan Nations meetings, because he sold a sawed off shotgun to an ATF agent. During a standoff at Weaver's home, Weaver's 42-year-old wife, 12-year-old son, and dog were shot dead by the FBI.

79 Hamm, *Apocalypse at Waco;* Stephen Jones and Peter Israel, *Others Unknown.* New York: Basic Books, 1998.

80 Louis Beam, "Leaderless Resistance," *Seditionist* (February 1992)12, http://www.louisbeam.com).

81 Jonathan White. *Terrorism: An Introduction,* 3rd ed. Belmont, CA: Wadsworth, 2002, p. 189.

82 Ibid., p. 190.

83 Alan Hart, *Arafat: Terrorist or Peacemaker?* London: Sidgwick and Jackson, 1984; Shaul Mishal, *The PLO Under Arafat.* New Haven, CT: Yale University Press, 1986.

84 Neil C. Livingstone and David Halevy, *Inside the PLO.* New York: Quill/William Morrow, 1990, p. 72.

85 David E. Long, *The Anatomy of Terrorism.* New York: Free Press, 1990, p. 36.

86 Ibid.

87 Laqueur, *No End to War,* p. 102.

88 Halevy and Livingstone, *Inside the PLO.*

89 It was during this occupation that the Phalange, under the control of the Israeli army, made its way into the Sabra and Shatila refugee camps in Beirut, supposedly to root out Palestinian gunmen. Instead, the Phalange massacred 460 to 800 individuals, 35 of whom were women and children.

90 Mishal, *The PLO Under Arafat.*

91 Kathryn Westcott, "Who Are Hamas?" BBC News. http://news.bbc.co.uk/1/hi/world/middle_east/978626.stm.

92 Buckley and Fawn (eds), *Global Responses to Terrorism: 9/11, Afghanistan and Beyond.* New York: Routledge, 2003, p. 157.

93 Clifford Simonsen and Jeremy R. Spinlove, *Terrorism Today: The Past, the Players, the Future.* Upper Saddle River, NJ: Pearson Prentice Hall, 2004, p. 341; Farc-ep. http://www.farcep.org.

94 Simonsen and Spindlove, *Terrorism Today,* p. 341.

95 Frank Stafford and Marco Palacios, *Colombia: Fragmented Land, Divided Society.* New York: Oxford University Press, 2002; Rachel Ehrenfeld, *Narco-Terrorism.* New York: Basic Books, 1992.

96 "Colombia's Most Powerful Rebels." BBC News. http://news.bbc.co.uk/1/hi /world/americas/1746777.stm

97 Simonsen and Spindlove, *Terrorism Today,* p. 341.

98 "Revolutionary Armed Forces of Colombia." Wikipedia. http://en.wikipedia.org/wiki/FARC.

99 Simonsen and Spindlove, *Terrorism Today,* p. 341.

100 "Revolutionary Armed Forces of Colombia." Wikipedia. http://en.wikipedia.org/wiki/FARC.

101 "Terrorist Organization Profiles From the ICT Database." Institute of Computer Technology. http://www.ict.org.il/inter_ter/org.cfm; Revolutionary Armed Forces of Colombia: People's Army. http://www.farcep.org/pagina_ingles.

102 J. Bowyer Bell, *The Secret Army: The IRA,* 3rd rev. ed. New Brunswick, NJ: Transaction, 1997; Toolis, 1997.

103 Steve Bruce, "Fundamentalism, Ethnicity, and Enclave," in Martin E. Marty and R. Scott Appleby, eds., *Fundamentalisms and the State.* Chicago: University of Chicago Press, 1993, pp. 50–67; Steve Bruce, "Paramilitaries, Peace, and Politics: Ulster Loyalists and the 1994 Truce," *Studies in Conflict and Terrorism* 18(1995): pp. 187–202.

104 White, *Terrorism,* p. 86

105 Ibid., p. 87.

106 Rhiannon Talbot, "Northern Ireland and the United Kingdom," in Frank Shanty and Raymond Picquet, eds., *Encyclopedia of World Terrorism.* Armonk, NY: M.E. Sharpe, 2003, p. 335.

107 White, *Terrorism,* p. 88.

108 Andrew Silke, "Rebel's Dilemma: The Changing Relationship Between the IRA, Sinn Fein, and Paramilitary Vigilantism in Northern Ireland," *Terrorism and Political Violence* 11(1999)1: pp. 55–93.

109 Simonsen and Spindlove, *Terrorism Today,* pp. 78–79.

110 Simonsen and Spindlove, *Terrorism Today,* p. 78.

111 Talbot, "Northern Ireland and the United Kingdom," p. 335.

112 Ibid.

113 James Dingley, "Peace Processes and Northern Ireland: Squaring Circles," *Terrorism and Political Violence* 11(1999)3: pp. 32–52.

114 White, *Terrorism,* p. 90.

115 Yossef Bodansky, *Bin Laden: The Man Who Declared War on America.* Roseville, CA: Prima Publishing, 2001; Ahmed Rashid, *Taliban.* New Haven, CT: Yale University Press, 2001.

116 Reeve, *The New Jackals,* p. 3. On August 27, 1998, the United States responded to the attack on the *U.S.S. Cole* by launching "80 Tomahawk cruise missiles from five warships in the Arabian Sea and two in the Red Sea," one to a pharmaceutical plant in Sudan, and another to a location in Afghanistan.

117 Ross, *The Dynamics of Political Crime.*

118 Jeffrey Ian Ross, ed. *Controlling State Crime,* 2nd ed. New Brunswick, NJ: Transaction, 2000; Jeffrey Ian Ross, ed.,

Varieties of State Crime and Its Control. Monsey, NY: Criminal Justice Press, 2000.

119 Townsend, *Terrorism,* p. 133.

120 Kathryn Westcott. 2002. "Who Are the Hizbollah?" BBC News World Edition, Thursday April 4, 2002. http://news.bbc.co.uk/2/hi/middle_east/1908671.stm.

121 "Who Are Islamic Jihad?" BBC News. http://news.bbc.co.uk/1/hi/world/middle_east/1005081.stm.

122 Kathryn Westcott. "Who Are Hamas?" BBC News. http://news.bbc.co.uk/1/world/middle_east/978626.stm)

123 Hoffman, *Inside Terrorism,* p. 27.

124 Hoffman, *Inside Terrorism,* p. 28; John Thomas Picarelli and Loise Shelly, "Methods Not Motives: The Convergence of International Organized Crime and Terrorism," *Police Practice and Review: An International Journal* 3(Winter 2001): pp. 305-318; Alex P. Schmid, "The Links Between Transnational Organized Crime and Terrorist Crimes," *Transnational Organized Crime* 2(1996)4: pp. 40–82.

125 Killyane, 1990.

Chapter 4
Terrorism Is Cyclical

126 The database can be viewed at: http://www.state.gov/s/ct/rls/pgf.rpt.

127 In June 2004, it came to the public's attention that the data presented in the 2003 annual report had serious problems and had underreported the amount of terrorism that occurred. The U.S. Department of State took responsibility, but argued, however, that in the interests of getting the report to the printer in time, data collection efforts were suspended before the year's end. On June 22, 2004 the revised database was released, and it is from this report the figures discussed in this chapter are drawn.

128 In June 2004, it came to the attention of the public that the data presented in the 2003 report had serious difficulties; apparently the amount of terrorism that occurred was underreported. The U.S. Department of State took responsibility. It argued, however, in the interest of getting the report to the printer in time, data collection efforts were suspended before the year end. On June 22, 2004, the revised data base was released, and it is from this report the figures discussed in this chapter are drawn.

129 Jenkins, *Images of Terror,* pp. 126–127.

130 MIPT Terrorism: Knowledge Base. http://www.tkb.org.

131 National Memorial Institute for Preventing Terrorism. http://www.mipt.org.

132 MIPT Terrorism: Knowledge Base. http://www.tkb.org.

133 Why is this the case? Israel, because of its seemingly nonstop conflict with the Palestinians, and the Americans, French, and British largely because of their transnational corporations.

134 MIPT Terrorism: Knowledge Base. http://www.tkb.org.

135 Jenkins, *Images of Terror,* 1979, p. 169.

136 MIPT Terrorism: Knowledge Base. http://www.tkb.org.

137 Jeffrey Ian Ross, "Beyond the Conceptualization of Terrorism: A Psychological-structural Model of the Causes of This Activity," in Craig Summers and Eric Markusen,eds., *Collective Violence: Harmful Behavior in Groups and Governments.* Lanham, MD: Rowman and Littlefield, 1999, pp. 169–194.

138 See for example, Jeffrey Ian Ross and Ted Robert Gurr, "Why Terrorism Subsides: A Comparative Study of Canada and the United States," *Comparative*

Politics 21(1989): pp. 406–426; Crenshaw, "How Terrorism Declines"; Ross, 1995.

139 Martha Crenshaw, "The Causes of Terrorism," *Comparative Politics* 13(1981)4: pp. 379–399; Jeffrey Ian Ross, "The Structural Causes of Oppositional Political Terrorism: Towards a Causal Model," *Journal of Peace Research* 30(1993)3: pp. 317–329; Jeffrey Ian Ross, "The Psychological Causes of Oppositional Political Terrorism: Toward an Integration of Findings," *International Journal of Group Tensions* 24(1994): pp. 157–185.

140 Ross and Gurr, "Why Terrorism Subsides."

141 Crenshaw, "How Terrorism Declines," p. 1.

142 Ibid., p. 12.

143 Ross, 1995.

144 Noam Chomsky, *The Fateful Triangle: The United States, Israel, and the Palestinians.* Boston: South End Press, 1983. This is not to say that it did not occur before this time.

145 James Chace. *Endless War: How We Got Involved in Central America-and What Can Be Done.* New York: Vintage Books, 1984.

146 David C. Rapoport, "The Four Waves of Rebel Terror and September 11," in Charles W. Kegley, Jr., ed., *The New Global Terrorism: Characteristics, Causes, Controls.* Upper Saddle River, NJ: Prentice Hall, 2003, p. 37.

147 Rapoport, "The Four Waves of Rebel Terror," p. 37.

148 Ibid., pp. 36–59.

149 Christopher Hewitt, "The Political Context of Terrorists in America," *Terrorism and Political Violence* 12(2000)3&4: pp. 338–339.

150 Weinberg and Pedahzur, *Political Parties and Terrorist Groups,* p. 21.

151 Sabri Sayari, *Generational Change in Terrorist Movements: The Turkish Case.* Santa Monica, CA: RAND Corporation, 1985.

Chapter 5
What Does the Future Hold?

152 See, for example, Graham T. Allison, *Nuclear Terrorism: The Ultimate Preventable Catastrophe.* New York: Times Books, 2004; Graham T. Allison, Owen R. Cote Jr., Richard A. Falkenrath, and Steven E. Miller, *Avoiding Nuclear Anarchy: Containing the Threat of Loose Russian Nuclear Weapons and Fissile Material.* Cambridge, MA: Belfer Center for Science and International Affairs, John F. Kennedy School of Government, Havard University, 1996; Raymond Zilinskas, "Terrorism and BW: Inevitable Alliance?" *Perspectives in Biology and Medicine* 34(1990); Jonathan B. Tucker, "Chemical/Biological Terrorism: Coping With a New Threat," *Politics and the Life Sciences* 15(1996): pp. 167–183; Jonathan B. Tucker, "Historical Trends Related to Bioterrorism: An Empirical Analysis," *Emerging Infectious Diseases* 5(1999):pp. 498–504.

153 Stern, *The Ultimate Terrorists.*

154 Reeve, *The New Jackals,* p. 258.

155 Judith Miller, Stephen Engelberg, and William Broad, *Germs: Biological Weapons and America's Secret War.* New York: Simon and Schuster, 2001.

156 Reeve, *The New Jackals,* p. 258.

157 Stern, *The Ultimate Terrorists,* p. 8.

158 Ibid., p. 66.

159 Ibid., p. 48.

160 Laqueur, *No End to War,* p. 227.

161 Ross, *Controlling State Crime.*

162 Ritzer, George, *The McDonaldization of Society.* Thousand Oaks, CA: Pine Forge Press, 2000.

163 See for example, Laqueur, *No End to War,* p. 220.

164 As of April 4, 2006, according to official sources, since the fighting began in Iraq, there have been 2,342 American military fatalities. Additionally, 103 British troops and 105 officers from other contries who have participated in the military operation have died (http://icasualties.org/oif). There are an estimated 33,821–37,943 Iraqi casualties (www.iraqbodycount.net).

165 Seymour Hersh, *Chain of Command: The Road From 9/11 to Abu Ghraib.* New York: Harper Collins, 2004.

166 Reeve, *The New Jackals,* p. 263.

167 Ibid., p. 264.

168 http://news.bbc.co.uk/go/pr/fr/-/2/hi/middle_east/298457.stm.

169 Ross, *Varieties of State Crime and Its Control.*

170 Chalmers Johnson, *Blowback: The Costs and Consequences of American Empire,* 2nd ed. New York: Henry Holt/Owl Books, 2004.

171 Naomi Klein, *No Logo: Taking Aim at the Brand Bullies.* Toronto: Vintage Canada, 2000.

172 Noemi Gal-Or, *Tolerating Terrorism in the West: An International Survey.* New York: Routledge, 1991.

Bell, J. Bowyer. 1997. *The Secret Army: The IRA,* 3rd rev. ed. New Brunswick, NJ: Transaction, 1997.

Buckley, Mary, and Rick Fawn, eds. *Global Responses to Terrorism: 9/11 Afghanistan and Beyond.* New York: Routledge, 2003.

Chace, James. *Endless War: How We Got Involved in Central America-And What Can Be Done.* New York: Vintage Books, 1984.

Chomsky, Noam. *The Fateful Triangle: The United States, Israel, and the Palestinians.* Boston: South End Press, 1983.

Crenshaw, Martha. "The Causes of Terrorism," *Comparative Politics* 13(1981)4.

Hutchinson, Martha Crenshaw. *Revolutionary Terrorism: The FLN in Algeria, 1954-1962.* Stanford, CA: Hoover Institution, 1978.

Johnson, Chalmers. *Blowback: The Costs and Consequences of American Empire,* 2nd ed. New York: Henry Holt/Owl Books, 2004.

Laqueur, Walter. *Terrorism.* Boston: Little, Brown, 1977.

Marshall, Chris. "Terrorism in Cyprus," in Frank Shanty and Raymond Picquet, eds. *Encyclopedia of World Terrorism.* Vol. 1. Armonk, NY: M.E. Sharpe, 1997.

Miller, Judith, Stephen Engelberg, and William Broad. *Germs: Biological Weapons and America's Secret War.* New York: Simon and Schuster, 2001.

Mishal, Shaul. *The PLO Under Arafat.* New Haven, CT: Yale University Press, 1986.

Ross, Jeffrey Ian. *The Dynamics of Political Crime.* Thousand Oaks, CA: Sage Publications, 2002.

———. "Post 9/11: Are We Any Safer Now?" in Lynne L. Snowden and Bradley C. Whitsel, eds. *Terrorism: Research, Readings, and Realities.* Upper Saddle, NJ: Prentice Hall, 2005.

———. "The Psychological Causes of Oppositional Political Terrorism: Toward an Integration of Findings," *International Journal of Group Tensions* 24 (1994).

———. "The Structural Causes of Oppositional Political Terrorism: Towards a Causal Model," *Journal of Peace Research* 30 (1993) 3.

Smith, Brent. *Terrorism in America: Pipe Bombs and Pipe Dreams.* Albany: State University of New York Press, 1994.

Stafford, Frank, and Marco Palacios. *Colombia: Fragmented Land, Divided Society.* New York: Oxford University Press, 2002.

Talbot, Rhiannon. "Northern Ireland and the United Kingdom," in Frank Shanty and Raymond Picquet, eds. *Encyclopedia of World Terrorism.* Armonk, NY: M.E. Sharpe, 2003.

Tucker, Jonathan B. 1996. "Chemical/Biological Terrorism: Coping With a New Threat," *Politics and the Life Sciences* 15 (1996).

Wardlaw, Grant. *Political Terrorism: Theory, Tactics, and Counter Measures.* New York: Cambridge University Press, 1982.

White, Jonathan. *Terrorism: An Introduction,* 4th ed. Belmont, CA: Wadsworth, 2003.

Wilkinson, Paul. *Political Terrorism.* New York: John Wiley, 1974.

Zilinskas, Raymond. "Terrorism and BW: Inevitable Alliance?" *Perspectives in Biology and Medicine* 34 (1990).

BOOKS AND ARTICLES

Crenshaw, Martha. "How Terrorism Declines," *Terrorism and Political Violence* 3 (1991)1.

Hewitt, Christopher. "The Political Context of Terrorists in America," *Terrorism and Political Violence* 12 (2000) 3 & 4.

Rapoport, David C. "The Four Waves of Rebel Terror and September 11," in Charles W. Kegley, Jr., ed. *The New Global Terrorism: Characteristics, Causes, Controls.* Upper Saddle River, NJ: Prentice Hall, 2003.

Ross, Jeffrey Ian. "Beyond the Conceptualization of Terrorism: A Psychological-structural Model of the Causes of This Activity," in Craig Summers and Eric Markusen, eds. *Collective Violence: Harmful Behavior in Groups and Governments.* Lanham, MD: Rowman and Littlefield, 1999.

Ross, Jeffrey Ian, and Ted Robert Gurr. "Why Terrorism Subsides: A Comparative Study of Canada and the United States," *Comparative Politics* 21 (1989).

Ross, Jeffrey Ian, and Reuben J. Miller. "The Effects of Oppositional Political Terrorism: Five Actor-based Models," *Low Intensity Conflict and Law Enforcement* 6 (1997) 3.

Schmid, Alex P., and A. J. Jongman. *Political Terrorism: A New Guide to Actors, Concepts, Data Bases, Theories, and Literature,* ed. New Brunswick, NJ: TransAction Books, 1988.

Weinberg, Leonard, and William L. Eubank. *The Rise and Fall of Italian Terrorism.* Boulder, CO: Westview Press, 1987.

Weinberg, Leonard, and Ami Pedahzur. *Political Parties and Terrorist Groups.* New York: Routledge, 2003.

WEBSITES

FBI Publications on Terrorism
http://www.fbi.gov/publications/terror/terroris.htm

Department of Homeland Security
http://www.dhs.gov/dhspublic/

RAND : Terrorism and Homeland Security
http://www.rand.org/research_areas/terrorism/

State Department—Counterterrorism Office
http://www.state.gov/s/ct/

page:

4:	Associated Press, AP	46:	Associated Press,
9:	Associated Press, AP		WHITE HOUSE
17:	Associated Press Graphics	50:	Associated Press Graphics
23:	Associated Press, AP	54:	Associated Press, AP
25:	Associated Press, AP	59:	Associated Press, AP
30:	Associated Press, AP	81:	Associated Press,
43:	Associated Press, AP		POOL NEW YORK TIMES

Cover: Associated Press, AP

JEFFREY IAN ROSS, Ph.D., is an Associate Professor, Division of Criminology, Criminal Justice and Social Policy, and a Fellow of the Center for International and Comparative Law, University of Baltimore. In 2003, he was awarded the university's Distinguished Chair in Research Award. He received his Ph.D. in political science from the University of Colorado. In 1986, Dr. Ross was the lead expert witness for the Canadian Senate's Special Committee on Terrorism and Public Safety. He created the first database on terrorism in Canada, which was later acquired by the Solicitor General of Canada. From 1995–1998, he was a social science analyst with the National Institute of Justice, a Division of the U.S. Department of Justice.

Dr. Ross is the author of *Making News of Police Violence: A Comparative Study of Toronto and New York City* (Praeger, 2000), and *The Dynamics of Political Crime* (Sage, 2002), and co-author (with Stephen C. Richards) of *Behind Bars: Surviving Prison* (Alpha Books, 2002). Dr. Ross is also the editor and co-editor of numerous books. His website is www.jeffreyianross.com.

LEONARD WEINBERG is Foundation Professor of Political Science at the University of Nevada. Over the course of his career he has been a Fulbright senior research fellow for Italy, a visiting fellow at the National Security Studies Center (University of Haifa), a visiting scholar at UCLA, a guest professor at the University of Florence, and the recipient of an H. F. Guggenheim Foundation grant for the study of political violence. He has also served as a consultant to the United Nations Office for the Prevention of Terrorism (Agency for Crime Control and Drug Prevention). For his work in promoting Christian–Jewish reconciliation Professor Weinberg was a recipient of the 1999 Thornton Peace Prize.

WILLIAM L. EUBANK is a graduate of the University of Houston, where he earned two degrees (B.S. and M.A.) in political science. He received his Ph.D. from the University of Oregon in 1978. Before coming to the University of Nevada, he taught briefly at California State University Sonoma and Washington State University. While at the University of Nevada, he has taught undergraduate courses in Constitutional Law, Civil Rights & Liberties, Political Parties and Elections, and graduate seminars in American Politics, the History of Political Science and Research Methods. The author or co-author of articles and papers in areas as diverse as statistics, research design, voting, and baseball, among other subjects, he is interested in how political violence (and terrorism) function as markers for political problems confronting governments.